I0487578

Creating A Remarkable Business Series

Part 1

The Entrepreneur's Handbook

Contents

Chapter 1 : Introduction

Entrepreneurs start a business with a fantastic idea, a vision which they want to realise, to bring into reality. Yet there is often the tendency to lose sight of your vision amongst the myriad day to day details. This handbook helps you to keep your eye on your big picture vision and to connect and align this with your immediate perspective, so that the many day to day activities that you and your team do, build and accumulate into the successful accomplishment of your vision.

In addition to knowing where you want to get to, another important aspect is having the 'fuel' to take you the distance, to your vision. The 'fuel' is supplied by you, it is your drive, determination and persistence to keep progressing towards your vision. Igniting your 'fuel' is your inspiration. You are naturally inspired to take action when a goal is of the utmost importance to you. Something is of the utmost importance to you when it is connected with your highest priority values. This handbook helps you to clarify your highest priority values and how to connect these values to your business vision.

This handbook also helps you to make sense of the different competing demands on you. You are the key element in your business as you provide the destination – your vision; the fuel to reach your destination; you are also the map reader, charting your route to your destination; in addition, you are also in charge of identifying the resources you need in order to expand your business so that you have the type of 'vehicle' which is appropriate to reach the destination that you have set. As your business grows you have the task of trying to seamlessly expand your business whilst at the same time keeping it moving forward. Where the different resources are not working smoothly together, the speed with which your business moves forward will slow down or even stall. You could even find that your business moves into reverse gear. The resources that we focus on in this handbook are the sources of value in a business: you; your customers; your team; your business processes and planning.

In Part 1, we look at your personal value system, your vision for your business and your financial goals. Your personal values, your business vision and financial vision provide the foundations from which you create and develop your unique business.

In part 2, we look at how your values and vision are translated to and embedded within your business. For example:

➢ Your value system significantly impacts on your business in terms of the brand values which you create, develop and communicate to your prospective and existing customers. Your value system also creates the culture which you embed within your organisation and how your employees interact and work with each other.

➢ The 'what' and 'why' of your business vision form the basis for preparing a more detailed vision for your business in terms of clarifying the structure, size and scope which would be capable of delivering your vision.

➢ Your personal financial vision is related to the financial goals which you set for your business. For example, the annual income from your business is physically paid out of the cash that your business generates. For your longer term financial vision you will be interested in the wealth or value which has accumulated in your business and which is ultimately realised when you step back from or sell your business.

Part 2 also provides an introduction to the key areas which an entrepreneur should be focusing on in order to create a remarkable business. These essential areas are then developed further in Parts 3 and 4.

Part 3 is concerned with connecting your long term vision (where you want to be and by when) with where you are now with your business. Bridging the gap between these two time periods and states is your business growth plan. We use and develop out a framework which gives you a step by step guide to help take you through the different growth phases of a business.

Part 4 is concerned with fine-tuning your business model and applies to each of the business growth phases which you choose to implement for your business. We look at those key areas of your business which often require continuous monitoring and fine tuning. The areas which we focus on are cash, profits and ongoing growth potential. These elements will often need much if not ongoing adjustment and refinement to create a resilient business over the short, medium and long term and to achieve the vision which you have in mind.

Chapter 2 : Vision

The entrepreneurial adventure starts with the business vision which you want to bring into reality - a big dream which you are truly passionate about. Your business dream is whatever you want it to be. You are in control of choosing both your vision and how you get there - the map is yours to create. It is essential to take the time to clarify what is in your mind's eye, both the essence of your ultimate goal as well as to scope out the detail - what this means in terms of the size, scale and scope of your future business which is capable of delivering your vision.

When you have identified your vision, you will need focus both to keep the big picture in your mind's eye and to act as a compass to keep you and your business heading in the right direction, towards your vision. You will also need persistence and a flexible plan to keep moving towards your vision as you will face many challenges, both internally — created by you and externally — from others, such as employees and competitors and others in the wider national and global environment.

Having a flexible plan helps you to cut through the maze of the many opportunities and challenges which come your way. Being absolutely clear on the long term vision that you want to achieve helps you to quickly sort through those events, possibilities and people which help you towards your goal, from those which will take you away from your goal or unnecessarily slow down your rate of progress.

Your long term vision can at times seem so far away that it is easy to lose sight of and belief in being able to realise it. Setting milestones along the way help you to see and measure your progress and to inspire you to continue onwards.

Chapter 3 : Talent

Introduction

The stories of the most successful entrepreneurs reveal that they have achieved their success in a variety of different ways. For example, success in different business sectors, such as Donald Trump in property and Bill Gates in computer software.

There are also examples of different entrepreneurs achieving success within the same sectors, such as Bill Gates at Microsoft and Steve Jobs at Apple, who both competed in the computer software market. Steve Jobs and Michael Dell competed with each other in the computer hardware market. Both pairs of individuals achieved their success using different business models.

One of the common threads linking these and other highly successful entrepreneurs is that they have built their businesses around their personal strengths and who have developed business models which allow them to continue to focus on what they are passionate about and most talented at doing.

This handbook provides a framework to show how you can create a strong, successful and truly remarkable business by working to your particular and unique set of values and strengths – what you are most passionate about realising and most talented at doing.

What are you talented at doing?

Aside from naturally knowing what you are talented at doing, one other approach to clarifying your particular talent is the Wealth Dynamics Profiling system. This profiling tool has been developed by Roger Hamilton especially for entrepreneurs. The profiling system recognises that wealth is created in many different ways and that each individual can maximise their talent-potential and wealth creation by focusing on one particular profile which accords with their particular source of talent. Wealth Dynamics can help you to both identify your particular source of creative talent and also in helping you to build a dynamic and creative team around you.

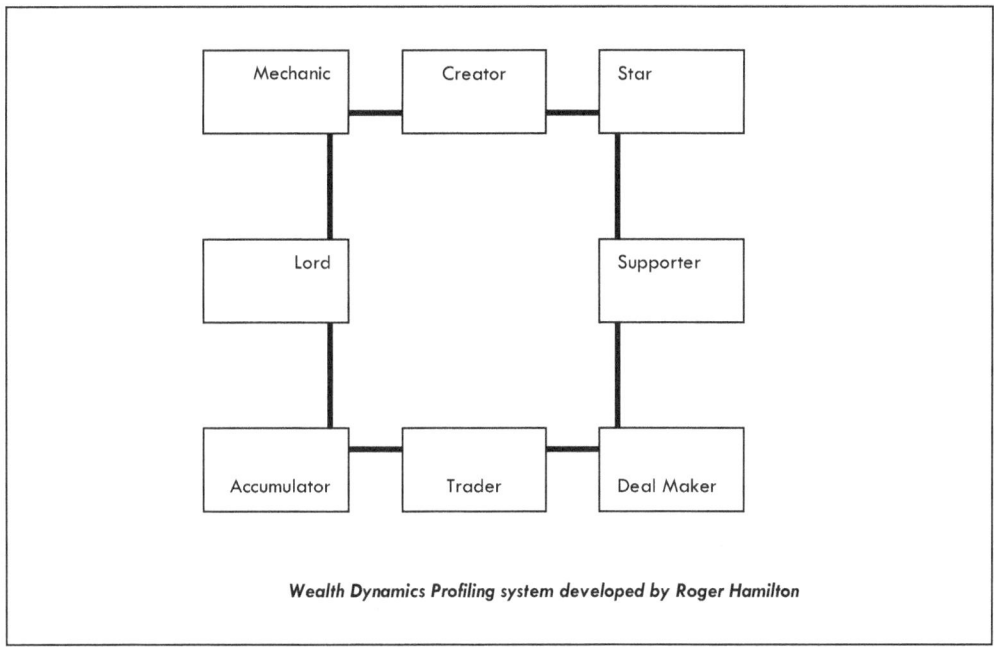

Wealth Dynamics Profiling system developed by Roger Hamilton

The Wealth Dynamics system identifies the following 8 different wealth creation profiles:

Creators create wealth through their ideas and in identifying gaps in the market or finding answers to the unmet needs of their customers. They are particularly skilled at taking their ideas and developing them into new products and services. For example, Richard Branson.

Stars create wealth through their brand. They are people who know precisely the values of their brand, what they stand for and also in how to not only effectively communicate these ideas and values to the world but also to inspire people into becoming their loyal customers. For example, Oprah Winfrey.

Supporters create wealth through their skill at leading and managing people and naturally inspiring and motivating them to work at their fullest potential. For example, Jack Welch at GE transformed the business into the world's second largest corporation.

Deal Makers create wealth through their negotiating skills and in recognising the opportunities around them to negotiate highly lucrative deals. For example, Donald Trump.

Traders create wealth through their skill at trading and in particular understanding timing - when it is both the right time to buy and also when it is the right time to sell to maximise their trading profits. For example, George Soros.

Accumulators create wealth through realising the capital growth value from assets. Assets may appreciate over time such as publicly quoted shares or from direct intervention in a business to maximise its potential for growth. For example, Warren Buffett.

Lords create wealth through the cash-flows generated from the assets that they own or manage. For example, Lakshmi Mittal in the steel industry.

Mechanics create wealth through developing efficient processes and systems. For example, Michael Dell, who with Dell offers customers the combination of an efficient system which allows them to customise their computer and at the same time to pay a competitive price. Creativity can also be in the scaling up of a business operation such as through franchising or licensing. For example, Ray Kroc in developing the McDonalds franchise.

Leadership

In addition to building a business around your talent, a successful business also needs strong and clear leadership. You are the creator of the vision for your business, only you know what you ultimately want to create and accomplish. You are also responsible for charting the course to take you and your business from where you are right at this moment in time to where you ultimately wish to be, or to arrive.

Charting your course, or creating and implementing your strategic plan, involves inspiring and motivating others to work with you to help you achieve your vision. Leadership is an active and continuous role, requiring consistent and ongoing communication of the outcomes you wish to achieve. Encompassed within your vision are the elements of not only what you want to realise but how you want to go about achieving it. The 'how' includes being clear on your brand — what do you want your prospective and existing customers to know about your products and services and how will they benefit from buying from you? and also in the culture you wish to embed within your business, such as how you and your team interact with each other within your business and also externally in the nature and strength of the relationships developed with your customers.

Chapter 4 : Action

Being a consistently successful entrepreneur involves taking action, that is being clear on what you want to achieve, creating a plan which takes you on the journey to arriving at your vision and in continuously working on achieving the goals you have set for yourself and your business.

Encompassed within 'taking action' is, on a consistent basis, taking the right kind of action at the right time. This includes a high level of awareness and understanding as to what is going on around you – what you can foresee and predict – in the wider environment, amongst your competitors, and in the internal 'beat' of your business. You will need good quality information which you can access on a timely basis about the many variables that can and do affect your business and its ability to thrive, especially in these highly uncertain times. Along with the awareness, understanding and analysis is the ability to make decisions and then to act decisively and to continue to assess and measure the outcomes of your chosen actions.

The entrepreneurial adventure is often a rollercoaster of a journey. You will be faced by ups and downs in running your business. There can also be seeming limbo times, where you don't seem to be making any forward progress. There can also be times when you seem to be in reverse gear and losing your grasp on the progress and growth you have made thus far. Your actions determine the direction your business goes in (forwards, backwards, limbo) and also it's speed along the direction that you have set in motion.

Both your business and the environment it operates in are dynamic, ever changing spheres of activity, where the pace of change continues to increase with ongoing globalisation. There will always be unforeseen events – either the event couldn't be predicted or the scale of the impact couldn't be predicted, such as with the global credit crunch. Your decisions and actions as to how you steer your business in reaction to such events will determine whether your business survives, thrives or dies. As the leader of your business you are responsible for the choices that you make: be it in the direction of survival (reacting with fear, an event is perceived as a problem or a threat), thriving (interpreting an event as an opportunity for your business), or exit (perhaps your business has been swept away by an event or you choose that you do not want to operate in a harsher environment).

PART 1 : Combining vision, talent and action — YOUR VALUES AND BUSINESS VISION

Chapter 5 : Your values and business vision

Introduction

In Part 1, we look at your personal value system, your vision for your business and your financial goals. Your personal values and your vision for your business provide the foundations or the core components from which you create and develop your business. Your personal values are unique to you, and as the owner of your business you embed your values into the business that you create which in turn creates a unique business. In addition, your vision for your business is unique to you where you are creating a business to accomplish a vision which you are truly passionate about.

The vision and values which we focus on in Part 1 are:

➢ Value System – what is important to you?

➢ Business Vision – what are you truly passionate about in accomplishing with your business?

➢ Financial goals – what amounts of financial income and wealth are important to you?

When your value system is closely connected to your business vision, that is you are truly passionate about accomplishing a big vision or a big dream then you will keep focused on the vision and will work persistently and relentlessly through and beyond the many challenges that you will encounter in your business. Where your values and your business vision are closely connected with your financial goals you will more readily identify the value of the products and services that your business sells and be focused on realising this value, such as in the prices you charge and in the profitability and other financial goals which you set for your business.

There is a balance and inter-connectivity to be found within these three elements: your personal value system; your vision for your business; and your financial goals. Without striking a balance on a consistent basis then you will encounter additional problems and challenges with your business which will significantly impact on your progress towards, and the ultimate accomplishment of, your vision.

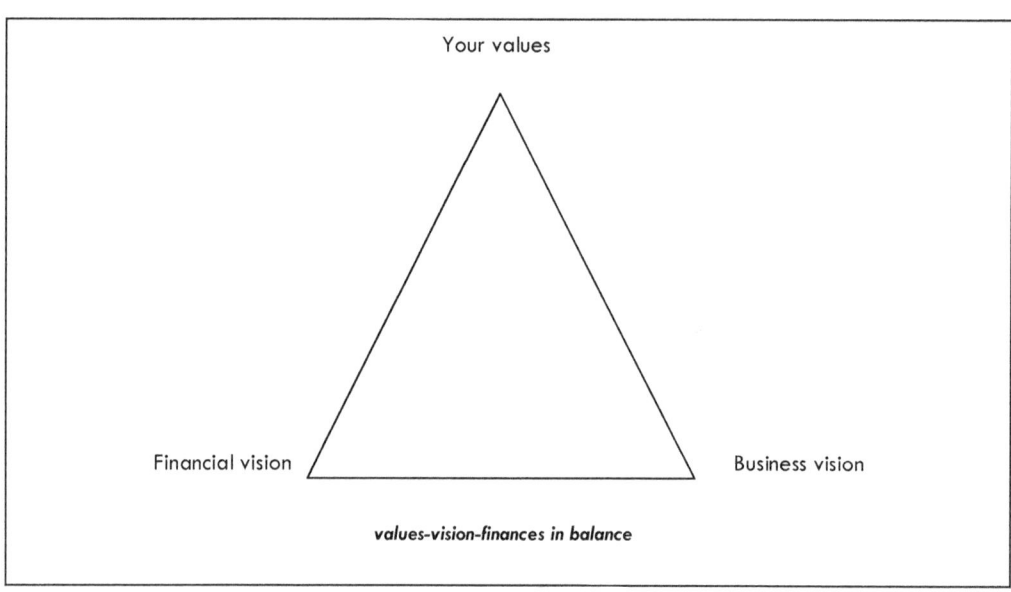

values-vision-finances in balance

Chapter 6 : Your value system

Introduction

One of the common factors amongst highly successful entrepreneurs is that they have built their businesses around their personal strengths, talent and values and have developed business models which allow them to continue to focus on what they are passionate about and most talented at doing.

In this chapter, we look at what 'fuels' you – what drives you to take action and to do the things that you do. In particular, we are looking at clarifying your own unique value system, that is, what is important to you and why.

What is important to you?

We will work persistently and relentlessly when we are either motivated or inspired to do so. What we are motivated and inspired by is based on our values. Our values are unique to each person and are based on our genes and our environment, by both the combination of nature and nurture. We are motivated and inspired by what is important to us. What you value highly impacts on how you see and experience the world around you and in what you filter into view and similarly filter out of view. What is important to you, you see, notice and respond to and what is a low or non-priority, you may well not even notice or recognise.

When you are inspired you are at your most focused and disciplined and you can muster up boundless reserves of energy and resourcefulness to achieve or to complete what you have set out to be, to do or to have.

When you are inspired into action you don't spend time procrastinating over whether or not to do something and you don't need anybody to persuade you to get involved, you automatically access your natural inner drive which propels you into action. Similarly, when you face a challenge in whatever you are inspired to accomplish, you don't have to think about whether to take on the challenge or not, you automatically take action and work at resolving it until it is overcome.

One framework which can be used to clarify what is important to you is the 7 areas of life. Identifying which of the 7 areas are important to you is the initial step, from which you can then identify the detail as to what specifically is important to you within each category which resonates with you. The answers that you come up with are unique to you, there is no right or wrong answer. Your specific interpretations form the basis of your unique value system.

The seven areas are:

➢ Spirituality: one interpretation is based on the thinking that each of us has our own unique mission or purpose in life which is deeply meaningful to us.

➢ Mental such as learning and personal growth and development.

➢ Vocational such as your work and/or career and what you are talented at doing within your working environment.

➢ Finances.

➢ Family.

➢ Social such as your friendships and your social networks.

➢ Physical such as your health, fitness and well-being.

These categories, although listed as separate items, are inter-connected. For example, your 'vocation' could also be your main source of generating financial wealth. In addition, the amount of time that you devote to your work affects the amount of your time available to spend on the other areas, such as time with your family.

Why is the 'what' important to you?

To look at, or to clarify, the 'why' behind the 'what' that is important to you, a helpful framework is Abraham Maslow's 'Hierarchy of Needs'. The basis of the model is that the "behaviour of an individual at a particular moment is usually determined by his or her strongest need". Maslow originally identified 5 needs which are shared by everyone, but each of us has our own particular blend of the 5 needs, with some needs being more important to us than others. The 5 needs identified by Maslow are as follows:

➢ Physiological: the basic need for food, shelter and warmth.

➢ Safety: the need for personal security.

➢ Social: the need to belong and to be accepted by various groups. The need for meaningful relationships with others.

➢ Esteem: the need to be more than just a member of a group. The need for esteem, both self-esteem and recognition from others.

➢ Actualisation: the need to maximise one's potential. This includes the 'need' to do what you 'love to' do and to fulfil a mission in life which you are passionate about realising.

In the Hierarchy of Needs theory, Maslow regarded that there was a general tendency for an individual to progress through the hierarchy of needs. For example, once you have satisfied one need, say a social need to belong then an individual tended to move on to the next level, that is to seek to satisfy a need for esteem, to stand out and be recognised by others.

However, Maslow also recognised that there were exceptions to this 'rule of thumb'. For example, inspirational leaders such as Gandhi and Dr Martin Luther King Jr had such great and far reaching visions, that their actualisation needs often resulted in their foregoing lower level needs, such as that of personal safety.

What is important to you and why changes both in the short term – temporary changes within your day and from day to day and also over the longer term. The changes are influenced by factors within you and also from the people around you as well as the wider environment.

Your values and your business

In terms of the more pertinent values for setting up your own business, since you can satisfy physiological, safety and social needs with most employed jobs, the higher level hierarchical needs are more likely to be the leading factors. For example, the need for esteem or recognition can arise where as an employee the prevailing work culture may not recognise and reward your work, skills and expertise. There may be actualisation needs where, for example, you have a personal vision which you are passionate about bringing into reality but which is not possible to start on, let alone to work towards realising within the context of an employed position.

That said, in the early days of proving your business and also when you face significant business challenges, you may be caught between 'physiological' and other lower level needs of earning sufficient income to cover your immediate financial commitments and the esteem and actualisation needs of accomplishing an inspiring business vision.

Positive and negative values

Each value which you have identified as important to you can act as both a positive and a negative force. The positive aspects serve as inspiration to propel you forwards to achieve whatever you have identified as important. The negative aspects can be found in any area of your life which is not working as you would like it to. The negative aspects have a source of fear, where the fear acts to hold you back, put you in limbo or to move you into reverse and away from achieving what you have identified as important.

Knowing what is important to you and why can help you, particularly when you are faced with challenges which affect you and your business. Being in business can often push you up to the edges of your comfort zone and far beyond, into the realm of fear and taking action when faced with a huge amount of uncertainty. For example, do you see challenge or opportunity in the current economy? Where are you on the spectrum of options – between becoming increasingly fearful for the future of your business and thus focusing on 'safety' needs and turning inwards to cut costs and trying to protect what you have created to date and in doing so you put on hold future growth plans and working towards your vision. Or alternatively do you feel confident that you have a strong business which can withstand whatever happens and thus you are inspired to look outwards to find those opportunities which will grow your business and take you closer to realising your vision?

If you are not getting the results that you want from your business on a consistent basis then you may be able to make some small changes in the perceptions you have about your values which can have a significantly positive impact on your results. For example:

➢ Look at whether you are taking action on what you have identified as important to you, or as is more likely, if you are being totally honest with yourself, you are avoiding taking action at all or avoiding the actions which you know will help you achieve what is important to you.

➢ The 'why' need that you have identified against your 'what' value may be one of the three lower level fear-based 'needs' (physiological, safety and social). Re-interpreting the need to an inspiration-based higher order 'need' (of esteem or actualisation) will change your perception as to the importance of the value you have identified. In doing so, you will be acting out of inspiration rather than fear and thus you will be more able to move forward and to deal with the challenges you are facing.

Comfort zone

We have a natural inbuilt default or protection instinct for stability and 'comfort', to stay as we are, even though the 'comfort' may be anything but. It is comfortable to the extent that it is a situation which we know and we understand the 'system' as it were, even though it may be a physically and/or mentally uncomfortable space to be in. Starting something new, such as starting a new business or taking your business through a new growth phase, involves moving out of your comfort zone. To keep moving forwards out of your comfort zone as easily as possible means keeping yourself inspired with the outcome which you are seeking to achieve. Your natural default of 'comfort zone' will return either when you've moved out of inspiration-mode and into fear-mode or when you've achieved your current goal. Seeking to achieve a big vision means that you will be continuously expanding your comfort zone as you work with and through fear and continue to inspire yourself to keep moving forwards to your vision.

Challenges you may face in the absence of clarity on your values

Some of the challenges which you may face with your business where you are not absolutely clear on what your personal value system comprises include:

➢ Lack of clarity in your brand message and one that does not set you apart from your competitors, leading to confused potential customers who are less likely to buy from you. This leads to lost revenue and also to lower potential profits as you are likely to be using a pricing system which does not reflect the unique value of your products and services.

➢ A lack of drive and desire to persist in successfully resolving challenges, which may ultimately defeat your business.

➢ Not prioritising your time to concentrate on working predominantly on those aspects of your business which you are talented at doing. Without prioritising, you are likely to spend too much time on those aspects which are not your particular strengths. One knock on effect can often be finding yourself drained of energy and momentum and over the long term you can lose sight of seeing your business as a fun and rewarding place to work. Another knock on effect is that you and your business will generate greater turnover when you spend more time working on what you are talented at doing. Spending less time doing what you enjoy and what you are good at results in lower turnover and a smaller business.

- ➤ If you lose energy and momentum with your business then this will very likely be noticed by your team of employees, who in turn, are likely to experience a fall in morale similar to yourself.

Chapter 7 : Your business vision

"The greater danger for most of us is not that our aim is too high and we miss it, but that it is too low and we reach it" (Michelangelo)

Introduction

Your business vision should be both big enough to inspire you on a daily basis to persistently and consistently work towards realising and also detailed enough to give you clear goals which you can focus on accomplishing, which step by step take you to your ultimate goal. This section looks at clarifying your big vision for your business. We look at the detail of your business vision in Chapter 12.

The essence of your big vision – the 'what'

What is the essence of your business vision – what is it that you are truly passionate about and committed to bringing to life via your business? The essence of your business vision should be a short sentence which encapsulates what you want to realise. A few examples might help to give you the flavour:

Bill Gates – to put a personal computer in every home and on every desk

Niklas Zennström and Janus Friis (founders of Skype) – "We wanted to provide free calling, and become one of the largest phone service operators in the world."

Distilling your vision down to a few words helps you to be absolutely clear what ultimate outcome or goal is required – there is very little ambiguity or vagueness in your sentence. Having absolute clarity in your wording helps you to not only keep the vision at the forefront of your mind but also grabs the attention, focus and interest of those who you share it with. The short but to the point vision helps you to quickly sort through the people who want to know more, within which you will find people who will positively go out of their way to give help and support and to connect you with the resources which you are looking for, such as contacts and investors.

Once you have arrived at a short but very precise description, check that this is really what you mean and that you are truly passionate about achieving the vision. In particular:

➤ Check that your wording covers everything which you have in mind. In other words, is your vision as big as you want it to be? Sometimes, you can create a short and snappy sentence but which is not everything that you have in mind. For example, the stated vision could be something smaller than what you are really passionate about on the basis that a smaller vision is going to be easier to accomplish than a bigger vision. However, a person is generally goal seeking – when a goal is set, they try to achieve it. In a sense a goal is a goal, whatever the size of it – a person will still try to achieve it, big or small. Also, the more impossible or audacious the goal may seem, the more likely you are to tap into resources and reserves that you didn't realise you had, because you've never found yourself in such a situation. In the words of Donald Trump "In truth you have more energy than you think you have. Most people are working at about 50% capacity. You can do much more. It takes a crisis or an emergency to get most people up to full steam".

➤ Also check that your statement is clear and unambiguous. When you state it to someone else, preferably someone who hasn't been involved in creating your vision, do they understand it straightaway or do you get lots of confused expressions and follow up 'what?' questions? The aim is to keep refining your short statement until it is 100% understood.

Your story – the 'why'

What is the story behind your vision for your business? Why are you so passionate about bringing your vision into actual reality? For example, you can review what has happened to get you to where you are today, such as:

➤ What you are talented at doing in a working environment.

➤ Your background, and in particular the key events which changed the direction of your life.

➤ Your previous career experience.

➤ What are the things you want to accomplish in and with your business but which you couldn't do in a previous job or business venture you have been involved in?

➤ If not all, then which aspects of your personal value system (identified in Chapter 6) are connected to your business vision.

Where you have a clear vision

Where you have clarity on both the 'what' and 'why' of your business vision, then you will find the following:

➤ You have a clear picture as to what you want to realise, which provides you with direction and focus. A clear vision gives you focus to keep working towards your vision and the necessary discipline and organisation to sort through the many opportunities which will come your way, such that you increase your chance of identifying those opportunities that are aligned with your business vision and which have the potential to speed you on your way.

➤ The energy and emotion that you have embedded in a clear vision will be readily apparent to those around you such as your employees and prospective and existing customers. Prospects and customers will be naturally drawn to and interested in what you have to say and to hear the belief that you have in your business and its products and services. When you are recruiting your team of employees, people will similarly be attracted to your business. Your inspiration will infect your team and similarly motivate and inspire them to positively work with you to realise your dream, they will go the extra mile – working longer hours than their contract requires and they will naturally do additional work without you needing to ask. In essence you create a highly motivated and focused team around you.

➤ Clarity in presenting your vision in a business plan which you may need to prepare where you are seeking outside investors. You have a vision which is easy for prospective investors to understand. Investors are more likely to invest in you and your business where they can believe in you, the owner and the vision that you are inspired by and highly driven to bring into reality.

Challenges you may face in the absence of clarity on your vision

Some of the challenges which you may face where you are not absolutely clear on what your business vision comprises, include:

➤ With no business vision you and your business could end up anywhere. Your business could well fail in its early years or survives by drifting along with a low growth rate or the growth rate plateaus when you have achieved the immediate goal of providing for your immediate financial requirements.

➢ There is less likelihood that your business dream embeds itself within your mind and instead your focus and activities are limited to fire-fighting the day to day activities.

➢ Where your vision is not aligned with your personal value system, you can give up on the vision, or downsize the scale and scope of it, when you hit the first few challenges. In these situations it can be quite easy for the challenges to sap your energy and belief in your long term vision and as such you may reduce the scale of your goals to achieving the immediate financial commitments you face.

Chapter 8 : Your financial vision

Introduction

A financial goal, as with any other goal or target which you set, identifies something specific which you want to achieve. With no goal in mind then you could end up anywhere. Just as you wouldn't leave home without knowing where you wanted to arrive at, then why wouldn't you set a monetary target which you wanted to achieve?

A monetary target can be especially tricky to create in terms of providing a meaningful goal, that is a goal which you will keep focused on working towards achieving. Monetary requirements often have an immediate time-frame and are a constant requirement whereas a business vision has a long term time frame, which can at times seem so far in the future that it can be blocked out by your immediate financial requirements.

In this chapter, the objectives are to identify and quantify two financial targets: the annual income and the long term value which you wish to realise from your business.

Annual income

What amount of money would you like to earn each year from your business? That is, the amount of money after deducting all relevant applicable taxes – the money that is yours to spend as you like.

The aim here is to calculate how much money you would need to earn from your business to support the lifestyle which you want to live and also for anyone else that you support financially. If you were to think about your ideal annual income and totally ignore any thoughts, of your own or anybody else's, that have the theme of 'you will never earn that much' and/or 'how on earth are you going to earn that much'.

Be specific, both in terms of identifying a number and also specifying – and being totally honest with yourself – what exactly are the items or people that you would spend the money on or the assets that you would invest the money in. This list could, for example, include your ongoing financial commitments and bills such as mortgage/rent, telephone and utility bills, school fees to the nicer things to spend money on such as holidays, clothes, car, gadgets, entertainment as well as any saving and investment plans which you have or wish to start contributing into.

You should be aiming to arrive at a financial value which is the total amount of money that you want to be able to pay yourself from your business which allows you to support the standard of living or lifestyle that is important and most meaningful to you. Such that being able to pay yourself this amount of money each year would leave you feeling fairly rewarded for all the persistence, risk, effort, energy and time which you have invested in your business and in building it into an even more valuable organisation over the course of the year.

Your list is not necessarily one that identifies hundreds of material items, such as a fleet of top of the range cars, yachts and houses. It should be a list of all the items you can identify which are important to have in your life and for which you will persistently work towards being able to buy for yourself and your family out of the money which you have earned, rather than borrowed from a third party bank or other financial institution.

Long term financial vision

Identifying your target long term financial vision is a similar exercise to that of the annual income calculations above. In this case, you are looking, using the best available knowledge which you have at your disposal currently, to arrive at a long term financial target which you would want to be able to realise at the time of achieving your vision or at some point subsequently when you look to step back from or to sell your business.

The long term financial value may represent the amount which you want to finance your retirement – which may be many years away or fast approaching, depending on your thoughts on what age you wish to retire from your business – some people want to retire as early as possible and some want to carry on for as long as they are able.

Alternatively, the long term financial value may represent, in part, the value you want to realise in order to fund your next business, if, for example you are a serial entrepreneur. The value could also include the more significant assets which you want as part of your lifestyle – the additional homes perhaps in luxury locations, a yacht, a fleet of sports cars. You may also be looking at funding more than your lifestyle, such as a charitable cause or other form of social contribution and cause which is important to you and which you are passionate about.

The objective is to identify, as far as you can, everything which you want to use the long term financial value to fund – write out a 'shopping list' for yourself, with the items which you want to include rather than items that you feel should be on there but which are not really that important to you.

Identifying items that are important to you and which are connected to your value system are ones which you are more likely to turn from being an imaginary 'shopping list' item and into a realised reality. These are items which are 'close to your heart' and therefore you have an in-built desire and motivation to acquire. In addition you are much less likely to forget about these items when the going gets tough with your business or where your long term financial goal seems so far away, compared with something that is nice to have but which you would not really push yourself to earn the money in order to be able to buy it.

In devising your long term financial plan it may be helpful to seek out the advice of an independent financial planning expert.

Chapter 9 : Linking values and vision

Introduction

So far, we have looked at 3 elements:

➢ Your values in terms of what is important to you and why.

➢ Clarifying what you are truly passionate about in realising with your business.

➢ Identifying the personal financial targets which are important for you to achieve.

In this Chapter, we first look at bringing these 3 elements together and identifying some of the problems which arise where there is an imbalance between these elements.

Values – vision – finances in balance

There is a balance and inter-connectivity to be found within the three elements: your personal value system; your vision for your business; and your financial goals. When your value system is closely connected to your business vision, that is you are doing work which is important to you and you are truly passionate about accomplishing a big vision then you will keep focused and will work persistently and relentlessly towards achieving it. You will work through and beyond the many challenges which you will encounter on your adventure and you will not stop until you have accomplished your vision.

Where your values and your business vision are closely connected with your financial goals you will more readily identify the value in the products and services your business sells and will be focused on realising this value, such as in the prices you charge, in communicating a compelling brand as well as in the profitability and other financial goals which you set for your business.

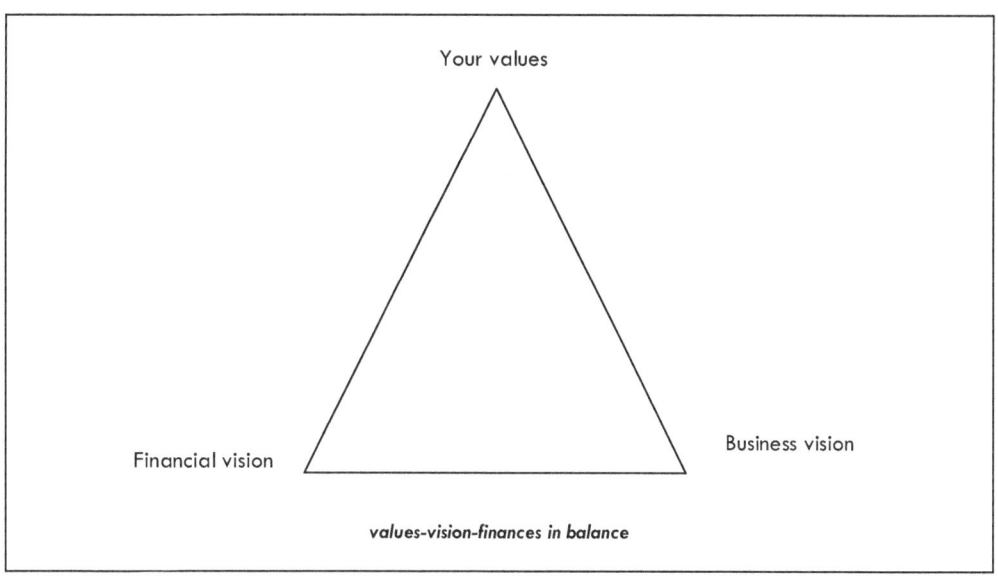

Your values

Financial vision

Business vision

values-vision-finances in balance

What can happen when there is an imbalance?

Without striking a balance on a consistent basis then you may encounter additional problems and challenges with your business which significantly impact on your progress towards your vision. The imbalances which you may experience comprise imbalances between:

➢ Financial vision and your values.

➢ Your values and your business vision.

➢ Your business vision and financial vision.

Financial vision and your values

There is an imbalance where financial income and wealth are not values which you regard as highly important to you. If this is the case, then in the absence of linking financial goals to those factors which you have identified as important then it is very unlikely that you will build and accumulate financial wealth and also you are unlikely to work to create a level of ongoing income to support the lifestyle that you want for you and your family.

Your values and business vision

There is an imbalance where your vision for your business is not aligned with your values. It is tremendously difficult to accomplish a vision for your business which you are not truly passionate about, since you are not tapping into your natural reserves of drive, determination and persistence to keep you focused on and working towards accomplishing a vision which may be many years into the future. In addition, the vision you set for your business may be much smaller than the vision that you would create if it was aligned with those values which are of the utmost importance to you.

Financial vision and business vision

The short term and immediate monetary requirements that you have can often, especially in the early days of your business, seem to be at odds with your long term business vision. A balance has to be struck, such as in the very early days in forgoing some financial reward as you lay the foundations of your business vision.

Where the financial vision consistently outweighs or blocks out the longer term business vision there is the significant likelihood that you will turn your focus away from working towards your business vision and instead focus on the constant immediate quest for financial income. The likelihood is that your business achieves the size and scale to support your immediate financial requirements but does not achieve either the big vision which you had in mind for your business or your longer term financial wealth goals. There is the tendency to find and do work which pays the bills rather than seeking out the quality of work which inspires you and the type of work which you had in mind when you first envisioned starting your business.

PART 2 – BUSINESS VISION AND VALUES

Chapter 10 : Integrating your values and vision with your business

Introduction

In part 2, we look at how the elements: your values, a business vision that you are passionate about and your financial goals are embedded within your business. In terms of our vision-values-finance diagram, we are now using the original diagram as the core and extending out each of these 3 elements to the corresponding areas within your business, as follows:

➢ Your value system significantly impacts on your business in terms of the brand values that you create, develop and communicate both to your prospective and existing customers and also in the culture which you embed within your organisation and how your employees interact and work with each other.

➢ The 'what' and 'why' of your business vision form the basis for preparing a more detailed vision for your business, in terms of clarifying the business structure, its size and scope, which would be capable of delivering your vision.

➢ Your personal financial vision is related to the financial goals that you set for your business. For example, the annual income from your business is physically paid out of the cash that your business generates. For your longer term financial goal you will be interested in the wealth or value that has accumulated in your business and which is ultimately realised when you retire from or sell your business.

Part 2 also provides an introduction to the key areas which an entrepreneur should be focusing on in order to create a truly remarkable business. These essential areas are then developed further in Parts 3 and 4.

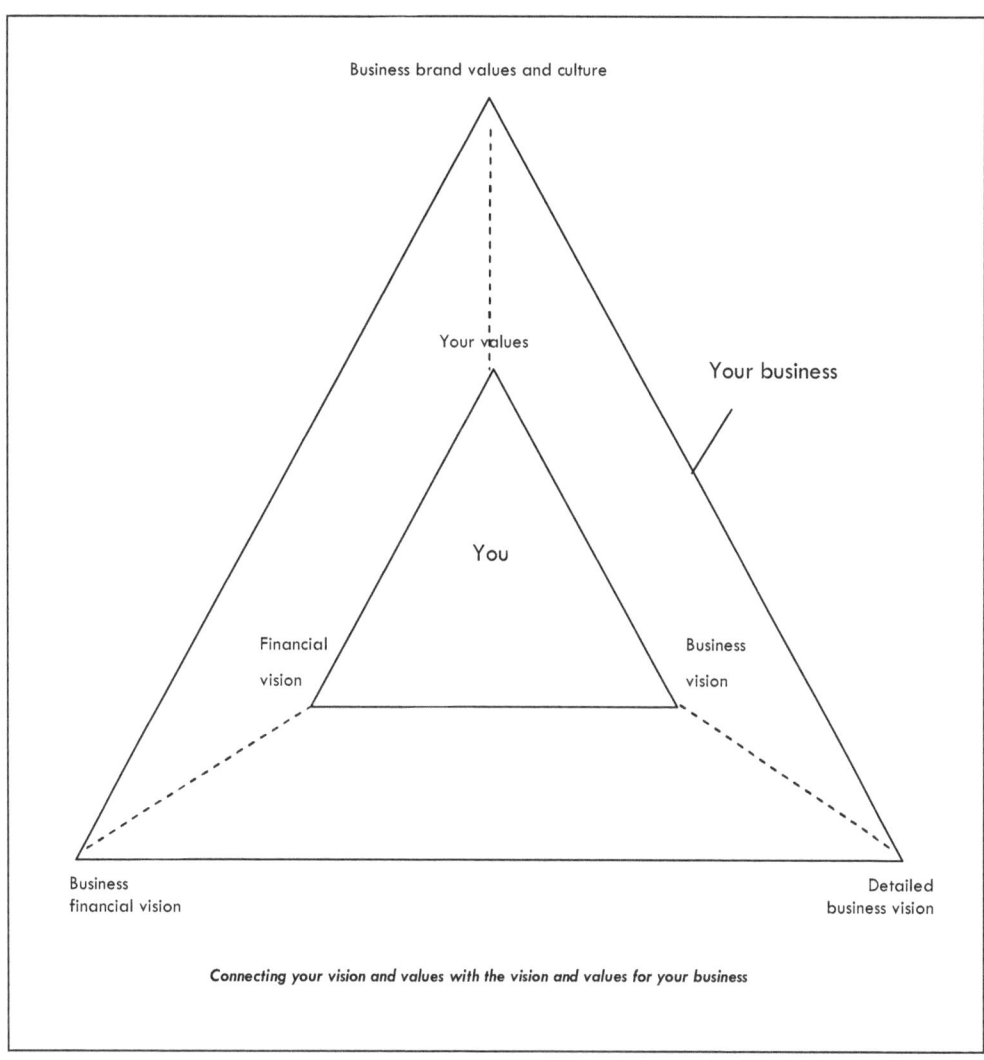

Connecting your vision and values with the vision and values for your business

Aligning your values with your business

When you have clarified what is important to you and why, you can then look at how these values are impacting on your business. Where you own your business and also work in it then you are likely to have the most significant impact on creating and developing the values of your business. Your values can, and most probably do, affect all areas of your business, whether or not you consciously sought to transfer or translate your values into your business. Some of the areas where your values influence your business include:

➢ Your business brand: your personality and values are embedded in the brand, or brand values of your business.

- ➤ Customers: your values impact on how you manage and develop customer relationships.

- ➤ Leadership and management: your values impact on how you motivate and inspire your employees to consistently work with you to achieve your vision and in the organisational culture you create.

- ➤ Finances: how you direct the use of your financial resources and the emphasis you give to generating cash, income, profits and growth within your business.

- ➤ Processes and systems: your values impact on the way things are done, and how products are produced and services delivered, including for example, the importance you place on quality, efficiency and communication between different groups or departments of employees.

- ➤ Planning: your values affect the emphasis you give to planning in terms of analysing results against expectations and implementing improvements and also in the time you take to plan for the future growth of your business and in seeking to reduce the downside risks to the actions you take.

Imbalances between brand and culture-business vision-financial vision

Where there are imbalances between the elements of your brand and culture, your business vision and your financial vision for your business then similar issues can arise as those noted in Chapter 9 with you personally, as within your business. For example:

- ➤ Misalignment between brand and culture and business vision can give rise to a brand and culture developing independently of your business vision such that your business does not realise the vision which you had in mind when you started your business.

- ➤ Misalignment between your financial vision and business vision could lead to a more predominant focus on finances at the expense of your vision, such as cutting costs and reducing expenditure. A business which spends too much time looking inwards and in cutting costs can rapidly lose touch with its customers and thus lose turnover and profits. Less focus and concern for your customers can result in lower growth and customers who can easily be persuaded to go to your competitors.

- ➤ Misalignment between brand and finances can lead to your sales team to make a sale at any cost, such as by heavily discounting. Such activities not only take value out of your brand on that sale but also in creating a customer relationship which encourages the customer to bargain heavily on cost and to interpret cost as the main influence in his buying decision rather than the benefits communicated in your brand message. The overall effect can be low profitability and low growth over the long term and a brand message which is either lost or not respected or valued by your team or by your customers.

Additionally, you need to involve everyone in your organisation in working in a balanced way and therefore you need to communicate, on a continuous basis, the balance you wish to achieve in the brand and culture of your business, the vision for your business and in the financial results required. Where an employee works in one particular area such as in the accounts department, then they need to know about the brand, culture and business vision so that they can understand where their work fits into your organisation, the manner in which you wish them to go about their work, that how and what they do impacts other people within your business and ultimately that they impact on the overall success of your organisation.

Chapter 11 : Brand and Culture

Introduction

Your value system significantly impacts on your business in terms of the brand values which you create, develop and communicate both to your prospective and existing customers and also in the culture that you embed within your organisation and how your employees interact and work with each other.

Brand

The term 'brand' can mean different things to different people. In this handbook we are looking at 'brand' in terms of understanding how your personal values are reflected in the brand which you create for your organisation – that is a corporate brand rather than the brand of a particular product or service. A corporate brand encapsulates the entirety of your business and covers the lifespan of your business. A corporate brand or brand personality starts with your personality and with the particular values which you embed within your business.

One of the best people to learn from in the sphere of corporate branding is Sir Richard Branson, the founder of Virgin. In his book Business Stripped Bare he explains that "brands exist as a means of communicating what to expect from a product or service – or to highlight the family likeness between different products and services". "The Virgin brand is a guarantee that you'll be treated well, that you'll get a high-quality product which won't dent your bank balance and you'll get more fun out of your purchase than you expected – whatever [the product or service] is."

"The Virgin brand came into existence gradually, to reflect what I was fundamentally interested in…my driving force, I realise now, was finding new ways to give people a good time – ideally in places where they were least expecting it. Like airports." Branson identifies those "powerful values of innovation, honesty, caring, value and fun." He believes that his brand is "about great customer service and giving people a good time."

A brand personality can be summarised as all the benefits to be derived by a user of your product or service and also about the nature of the service they will receive from your business. In terms of your values, what you have identified as important to you contains the seeds of the unique elements about your business which can set your brand apart from that of your competitors. For example, your brand message should include the following elements:

➤ Referring back to your personal values (Chapter 6), what is important to you in how you do things, for example in how you treat your customers and in the quality of relationships you build with them?

➤ What is important to you in the quality of the products and services that you provide, such as in their technical precision or that your products consistently deliver on the promise that you make in terms of the benefits received by customers or in the problem that your products and services solve.

➤ You can also draw on the Maslow Hierarchy of Needs in communicating 'why' customers should buy from you. For example, in Taking Brand Initiative, Hatch and Schultz use BMW as an example in terms of using "brand symbolism [to help] people to identify others with similar values or interests (the basis of belonging) while at the same time differentiating them from people with dissimilar interests." The Maslow needs identified here are both social (belonging) and esteem (differentiation). The corporate brand of BMW "welcomes employees, customers and other stakeholders into its extended family and also differentiates BMW from competitors who simply make cars."

➤ Communicating the above elements in your brand message consistently across all your sales and promotional materials, website and any other areas where you are communicating your brand message to an external audience as well as in the words, behaviours and attitudes of your sales team when they are working with your customers.

➤ Continuously honing your brand message so that you communicate to your customers in a way which is compelling to them and thereby you attract those customers who also highly regard your particular set of highlighted values.

Culture

The culture of a business can be neatly summed up in the phrase 'how we do things around here'. The culture of a business is created and embedded by you, the owner of a business in terms of how you do things, be it in producing your products and services, how you interact with your customers, how you interact with your employees, and also in what you don't do or say. The way you do and don't do things is picked up on by your employees as they work out what is the required behaviour to have in your business.

The Cultural Web, developed by Johnson and Scholes identifies 6 elements which make up an organisation's culture and explains how you do things in your business:

➢ Stories: the stories told by you and your team to each other and to outsiders embed the present in its organisational history and also highlight important events and personalities such as successes, failures, heroes and villains. They distil the essence of an organisation's past, legitimise types of behaviour and are devices for telling people what is important in the organisation. Who and what a business chooses to immortalise says much about what it values and perceives as the way to behave.

➢ Rituals and routines: the daily behaviour, actions and activities of people that signal the expected behaviour and what is expected to happen in given situations and what is valued by management.

➢ Symbols: symbols can be as varied as logos, offices, cars and titles and the type of language used.

➢ Organisational structure: the organisational structure is both the formal organisational chart – how employees are organised as well as the less easy to spot real sources of power which often do not match up to the organisational chart.

➢ Control systems: the control systems are the measurements and reward systems implemented by senior management – in effect what is considered important by management is what gets measured. For example, to earn bonuses and commission your team will adopt those behaviours that seek to achieve the highest rewards and these may well be at odds with the brand message you are seeking to communicate.

➢ Power structures: the real areas of power in a business – this may be a particular group within an organisation such as the marketing department or finance department.

All of the above elements combine to create the mindsets, behaviour and atmosphere that are the culture and values of your organisation.

The culture of your business starts with your personality and the traits and values which you seek to embed within your business and your team of employees. You embed your values and personality in the culture of your organisation in many ways, such as in:

➢ The training and development of your team.

- The delegation of tasks to your team and entrusting them to complete tasks in the absence of both micro-management from you and in your team delegating the same tasks back to you.

- Your review of the quality of work done and the way in which you give feedback.

- The formal appraisal systems which you implement in your organisation.

- What you choose to incentivise your team to perform well at.

- How you regard and treat customers and others external to your business.

Imbalance between brand and culture

Where you are clear on your value system and apply your values in the same and consistent manner with your team and your customers then there should not be an imbalance between the brand of your business and the culture you create within your organisation.

However, imbalances often arise and in Taking Brand Initiative by Hatch and Schultz, the imbalance can be summed up in a difference between 'who we are' (the culture of an organisation) and 'how others perceive us' (how customers and other 'outsiders' perceive an organisation).

An imbalance can present itself in a number of ways, for example:

- An organisational culture that is inwardly focused, where your employees are more concerned with office politics than in serving their customers.

- Customers do not consistently receive what is promised in your brand message, such as a product or service that doesn't give the results that it is supposed to, or in customer service which provides little if any service at all as perceived by customers.

- An organisation which is more concerned with pushing the boundaries of the functionality of its products when more functionality is not needed by customers.

- Little involvement and interaction with customers so that your organisation is out of touch with the ever changing needs of your customers.

- A high rate of lost customers each year which can translate into lower turnover where you cannot replace previously loyal customers with new ones at a fast enough rate or with ones which spend at least the same amount of money with you. Lower profitability can also result where you spend more money to obtain a new client than you did to retain a once loyal customer.

Chapter 12 : Detailed Business Vision

Introduction

In this chapter we return to the business vision which you set out in its essence in Chapter 7 and add in the layers of detail which help to make your vision more tangible and connected to reality. The aim is to build as detailed a picture as you can so as to see what the business behind your vision could look like.

Detailed business vision

With a detailed business vision, the aim is to create a picture of the business and business structure which you would need to have in place in order to be able to deliver the big vision you have in mind. What might your business look like in reality? In addition, by when do you want to achieve your business vision? That is, by what specific date do you want to fully realise your vision for your business?

Returning to the examples in Chapter 7, with either Bill Gates' vision or Niklas Zennström and Janus Friis of Skype's vision you can see the actual size and scope of the business and business structure which supports the vision that they have each realised. For example, you can look at the financial statements of their organisations, their websites and even take a look at their office and operating locations. In looking at what you want to realise you can often find a number of organisations, some perhaps in totally unrelated business sectors which have accomplished a size of vision that you have in mind.

Writing down your vision in as much detail as you can has the effect of starting to make your vision a reality. In addition, writing down what is in your mind has the effect of downloading the scene or scenarios that you have been developing, and once it is written down you then free up space in your mind to further develop what you have created to date. Developing a detailed picture of your vision takes time and numerous attempts at refining what you have in mind. You will naturally know when you have reached the end of your refinements when you intuitively feel that the picture is complete and you have nothing more to add or not until you have started working towards realising your vision and you have actual data and results to compare with the goals that you originally set for you and your business.

Spending time on developing the detail of your vision and in the meticulous building of layer upon layer of information helps to embed the vision or dream in your mind and thus increasing the probability that the picture will remain at the forefront of your mind, rather than something that is forgotten as time goes by.

Set out below is a list of some of the questions or issues to consider in order to help you to develop a clear and detailed picture as to what you envision your business comprising in terms of its structure, size and scope at the time that you accomplish your vision:

You – as the business owner

➢ What role do you see yourself playing in your organisation? For example, a managing director role which involves spending the majority of your time directing the business on its long term course; a hands-on role working with your specific talent e.g. sales, marketing, product development; or a part-time role which also allows you to work outside the business on other interests.

➢ What are you passionate about in the context of your business?

➢ What skills and competencies do you bring to the business, what are you most talented at doing?

➢ What values do you wish to highlight in your brand and embed in the culture of your business?

Your customers

➢ Which geographical markets will your business be operating in e.g. worldwide, nationwide, locally?

➢ What products and services do you envisage selling? At this point in time it is an unknown as to what exactly your entire product and service range will be at the future date that you have in mind for realising your vision. For now, consider how far you can extend your current range of products and services. For example new products and services which could potentially complement your existing range as well as considering how far you can extend your customer base who have a need for your products and services.

➢ Which markets will you be selling in? business to business (B2B), business to consumer (B2C) or both?

➢ Which business sectors and/or niche markets will you be operating in?

- Consider the potential for additional growth coming from joint ventures or partnerships with other organisations.

- Consider the potential for franchising your business model or licensing your products and services as additional methods for growing your business.

- What do customers buy from you, in terms of the perceived benefits that your products and services provide? What customer needs are you seeking to fulfil with your products and services?

- What is your corporate brand? What values and personality do you wish to embed within the brand of your business and in the products and services your business offers?

- What will the nature of your customer relationships be? how do you see your team interacting with customers, for example, customer service with a high level of involvement and interaction between your employees and your customers, or a focus on lower personal involvement, perhaps a relationship provided via a predominantly internet based service?

People – your team

- Broadly, how many people will there be in your organisation e.g. 50, 100, 1,000, 10,000 or more. As a rough guide, perhaps you can find an existing organisation of a similar size that you have in mind for your business and look at their accounts to see how many people they employ.

- What type of organisational structure will you have? For example, functional departments such as marketing, finance and sales departments. What roles and responsibilities will your key members of staff have?

- What building space do you need? one building where all activities are carried on, a building in each geographical location which you operate in, perhaps different sites in different countries as you develop a low-cost and efficient global supply chain.

- What will the internal office culture be? what are the mindsets, behaviours, values and atmosphere that you wish to create and develop within your organisation.

Processes and systems

- Logistics: how will you organise the efficient production and delivery of the products and services you sell? For example, a low cost worldwide production and delivery system;

finding efficiencies in the mix of standardised and bespoke products and services that you offer your customers.

➢ What is your system for research and development? – getting ideas, developing these ideas, testing them out in the market and delivering a new product or service to the market. How will you organise the communication of these ideas from the idea generators (such as yourself, your sales and marketing teams, your customers) into products (your production team, operations department)?

➢ What significant fixed/physical assets do you need, such as plant and machinery, computer software and hardware?

In helping you to add the detail to your business vision, you can also look at real-life examples of existing businesses. The examples may not necessarily be in the same competitive niche or business sector. Some useful areas to look at may be those businesses which have developed and grown over a similar time-scale that you have in mind for your vision and who have also achieved a similar size and scope that you have in mind. You can also look at those organisations which you consider to be led by charismatic leaders which you feel some affinity with – which leaders have inspired you?

Chapter 13 : Business Financial Vision

Introduction

Your personal financial vision is related to the financial goals which you set for your business. For example, the annual income from your business is physically paid out of the cash which your business generates. For your longer term financial goal you will be interested in the wealth or value which has accumulated, via profits and growth, in your business over the course of its development.

Cash

The immediate viability concerns of your business are determined by your cash balances and cash flows, such that if you run out of cash then your business can cease very quickly without an injection of funds to cover the shortfall. Without a good understanding of how your business generates and uses cash, that is the stock of cash (the balance in your business bank account) and the flows – in their timing and magnitude - you can never really be sure of the viability let alone the strength and sustainability of your business over the longer term.

A viable business model is one which generates cash from its ongoing business activities that meet the expenses required to produce goods and services, as well as allowing you to pay yourself the level of annual remuneration which you seek from your business (the amount identified by you in Chapter 8) and also allows you to reinvest funds within your business to help to finance its future growth.

Profits

The profits of a business take on a more short and medium term time frame, compared with the immediate importance and viability attaching to the cash which your business generates. The profits are the paper flows, arising from the difference between sales invoices generated and purchase invoices received together with non-cash or accounting adjustments such as depreciation for a particular time period.

You will need a good understanding of the profits profile of your organisation. For example:

➢ The gross profit margin: turnover minus costs directly involved in producing your goods and services gives you your gross profit. The gross profit divided by your turnover and expressed as a percentage gives you your gross profit margin.

➢ The net profit margin: turnover minus all revenue costs attributable to the period of time under review gives you your net profit, which is also termed 'net profit before tax'. The net profit divided by turnover and expressed as a percentage gives you your net profit margin.

➢ The tax rate levied on your net profits after adjustment for tax rules.

➢ What turnover and profits do you need in order to be able to withdraw the level of income which you wish to receive?. The tax effects of salary and dividends can be provided by your accountant.

➢ What profits remain after taxes, costs and your remuneration which is available to reinvest in your business?

➢ You can benchmark your profits profile against other organisations within your industry to see both where your business is performing better and also to identify areas where you may be able to identify ways to improve the profitability of your business.

Some of the key factors which affect the profits and profitability of your business are:

➢ Pricing.

➢ Efficiency.

➢ Costs.

Pricing

The pricing of your products is often the most important factor in the profits and profitability of your business. Pricing can also be a highly emotive issue for the person or team involved in setting a price, for which, you, as the owner of your business are ultimately responsible for. Their can be fears that increasing a price would result in a mass loss of your customer base.

Getting a greater understanding of pricing revolves around identifying the value which your customers place on your products and services. One aspect of value is price, but you need to know how important a factor price is amongst your customers (and prospective customers) compared with the benefits and attributes which they perceive to receive in using your products and services. You should also compare how your products and services fare against the value which your customers and potential customers perceive to be on offer from your competitors.

Efficiency

The utilisation of your key income producing assets impacts on your profitability. It can be fairly straightforward to measure the efficiency of a piece of equipment but often less so where your key assets are your employees (unless you use a time recording system). The aim is to find a consistently high rate of utilisation which does not regularly push assets or people into over-capacity i.e. having too much work to do in the time available.

Efficiency applies to any system within your organisation, for example, your system for generating sales, for retaining customers, for cash collection. The efficiency of any particular system can be measured and understood when you use a formal system, that is, one which is followed by every relevant employee.

Costs

The absolute size of your costs affects the level of profits and profitability of your company. The lower are your costs then the higher are your profits. The type of cost is also relevant, whether the expense is a variable cost or a fixed cost. A variable cost is one that varies with the level of production or service delivery. For example, if you sub-contract part of your production, such as using sub-contract labour then you would only incur the cost of the labour should you have an order in place and no expense where you have no order. A fixed cost, such as an employee's salary, is one that you have to pay whether or not you have an order to produce or a contract to deliver.

Growth and innovation

The growth rate of your business impacts on the finances of a business over the medium and long term. Growth can be organic, with ideas, new products and services being created and developed from within the business. Growth, especially rapid growth can also come from external sources, such as from acquiring another business. Growth can come from incremental improvements and extensions to your existing range of products and services. Additionally, growth can come from innovations which cause a dramatic change in the industry you currently operate within or from creating a new industry segment, both of which can provide sources of dramatic growth for your business.

Vital to the growth of a business is knowledge and understanding of the needs and requirements of your customers, both in what they are looking for now and also in the future. As an organisation grows and more levels of structure are added, be it distinct departments within an organisation or different offices spread over an increasing number of geographical locations, relaying information about new customer needs and new ideas created within the organisation, becomes increasingly difficult unless there are clear communication channels to disseminate and discuss ideas.

Longer term valuation

In seeking to achieve the long term personal financial goal which you identified in Chapter 8 you will be dependent on the value accumulated in your business. In particular, either the value which a 3rd party is willing to pay to acquire your business (where you are seeking to ultimately dispose of your business) or the value calculated by an independent valuer (where you are perhaps looking at your business or other connected party to buy out some of your shares in return for a lump sum, which could be the case where you are stepping back from your business but which you wish to retain some involvement, or even control, at the shareholder level).

Company valuation

In terms of scoping out the boundaries of an initial estimate of a valuation for your business, a first step is to find out if there is a common valuation method or 'rule of thumb' used for your particular industry and secondly to find out whether there is a commonly used multiple factor. For example, two common valuation methods are a multiple of turnover or revenues and a P/E or price/earnings multiple.

Returning to Chapter 12, where you looked at other organisations to get an idea of the size of business that would be capable of delivering your vision, you will have an idea of one or several financial targets to aim for. One financial target which you can use as a starting point for your valuation estimate is the turnover of the organisations which you looked at, or perhaps an average of the turnover figures you noted.

Turnover or revenue multiple

This valuation method is simple and easy to work with in order to calculate an initial valuation for your business. An initial calculation would be simply to multiply the rule of thumb industry multiple by the turnover estimate which you have in mind for your business.

There are likely to be some other adjustments to fine-tune your estimated valuation and on which a business valuation expert would be able to advise you.

Price/earnings multiple

In the absence of a 'rule of thumb' price/earnings or P/E multiple for your industry you can often find a guideline figure from the financial pages of a newspaper. The financial pages provide a P/E multiple for each publicly quoted company with the data being organised by industry sector. The P/E multiple for a business reflects its future growth potential as estimated by external investors and financial market analysts.

Using an estimate of a P/E multiple based on a publicly quoted company can only provide a very rough guide to the potential valuation of a private business (that is one that is not quoted on a recognised stock market). However, making an initial calculation of a business valuation does provide a starting point which can be refined over time.

Where you have a P/E multiple estimate then you would multiply this multiple by the profit after tax figure of your organisation to give you a calculation of the valuation of your business. There are then some further calculations and estimates to use where you have a turnover figure in mind, in order to work your way from the turnover to the profit after tax figure. The additional estimates that you would need are in respect of your costs and tax liability. To simplify these calculations you could use an estimate of the percentage of costs and tax. An example is shown below (page 50), which uses a turnover figure of £10 million, an estimate of cost of sales of 40% of turnover, other costs representing 40% of gross profit, tax of 30% of net profit. An estimate of the P/E multiple is 10 and the business owner holds 75% of the shares of the organisation. The example gives a business owner share of the valuation of £18.9 million (before personal tax).

Profit and loss account extract	Notes	Example	£
Turnover			10,000,000
Cost of sales	Direct costs of producing your products and services	40% x turnover	(4,000,000)
Gross Profit			6,000,000
Other costs	Other costs including your salary	40% x gross profit	(2,400,000)
Profit before tax (net profit)			3,600,000
Tax		30% x profit before tax	(1,080,000)
Profit after tax (PAT)			2,520,000
Business owner valuation for a 75% holding	P/E of 10 x PAT x 75%	10 x 2.52m x 75%	**18,900,000**

Estimate of a business valuation using a P/E multiple

Where you have estimated a total valuation for your organisation from using the turnover multiple or a price/earnings multiple or are using another valuation method which is more appropriate for your business sector, then the following additional adjustments would be required to calculate an estimate of your share of the financial value of your business, as follows:

➤ Apportion the value in respect of the percentage shareholding that you own directly.

➤ Adjusting the valuation upwards for an estimate of inflation over the period between now and the time period you have set to realise your vision.

With regard to your long term financial goal, you have scoped out an initial estimate above in order to identify your initial financial boundary. Over time, as your business grows and achieves or exceeds the financial targets which you have set, then it can be worth obtaining expert help to add more clarity and refinement to your initial estimates. The expert help could, firstly be from a business valuation expert who can help you with advising on the finer detail of a valuation of your business. Secondly, seeking help from an accountant who can convert a business valuation into an estimate of the amount you would receive, after taking into account factors such as other shareholdings not held directly by you and tax implications. Any financial valuations would need to be regularly reviewed, such as at the time that you are moving on to the next growth phase for your business since the basis for the valuations may have changed, such as tax rules and prevailing industry valuations for your business.

PART 3 – CONNECTING YOUR LONG TERM VISION TO THE HERE AND NOW

Chapter 14 : Vision Goals

Introduction

Part 3 is concerned with connecting your long term vision (where you want to be and by when) with where you are now with your business. Bridging the gap between these two time periods and states is your business growth plan. We use and develop out a framework which gives you a step by step guide to help take you through the different growth phases of a business.

The framework we use comprises the following elements:

➢ Your vision goals (Chapter 14).

➢ Where you are currently in terms of achieving these goals (Chapter 15).

➢ Identifying the gap between the above two boundaries, between where you want to be in terms of your vision and where you are now and then bridging the gap with the different growth phases which you can take your business through (Chapter 16).

➢ Using key milestones, time periods and financial targets for each growth phase to connect where you are now to accomplishing your vision (Chapter 16).

➢ Within each growth phase, using the combination of the sources of value: you, your customers, your team, processes and systems and planning, which create your unique business (Chapter 17).

Vision goals

The starting points for identifying your vision goals, are the long term goals which you wish to ultimately achieve with your business, as identified in Chapter 12 and the long term valuation you wish to realise from your business, which you identified in Chapter 13.

In developing the detail of your business vision in Chapter 12 you were in a sense writing the story of your future business – a rich and detailed picture which you are able to envision at this stage. Your vision goals are the summary points for each specific area of your vision that you identify. A framework which you can use is shown on pages 55 and 56.

In order to set the long term financial goals for your business, you can use the valuation, turnover, gross profit margin and the net profit margin data which you estimated in Chapter 13. As your business develops, consider seeking out a formal business valuation from qualified experts. Any valuation can only be an estimate until someone formally approaches you with an interest in acquiring your business. Even then the ultimate price would only be found after a negotiation.

Each of the vision goals which you identify should be specific and measurable so that you know when you have accomplished the goal. A goal which is vague and can be interpreted by you in different ways or by different people in different ways needs to be re-defined until it is unambiguous. Numerical and financial targets are usually unambiguous. However, it may seem less straightforward in identifying unambiguous qualitative goals. For example, setting a goal for customer relationships could include numerical measures, such as how long do you wish customers to remain buyers of your products and services. Is there an average customer lifetime period for your industry? The nature of the relationship you wish to develop with your customers should be measurable. Whatever it is that you wish to measure can then be developed out into a customer questionnaire which either your business or an independent third party can use to measure how well you are doing. Additionally, the factors that you wish to measure should also be important factors for your customers, or the customers that you wish to develop long standing relationships with. The important factors for your customers will be those that strongly influence their decision to buy from you, such as the perceived benefits and unmet needs which are being satisfied by using your products and services. Different influences are likely to be identified by different customers and where the same influences are identified there can often be a range of importance or significance attaching to the identified buying factor. The information that you can gather on buying decision criteria can be used as the basis for segmenting your customers that is, identifying groups of customers with the same buying criteria. From that basis you can gather more customer information from your own records to ascertain your key customer groups, such as those who contribute the most turnover and/or profits to your business. The data you have assembled can then be used in your future sales messages as you know which factors are the key ones in attracting the type of customer that you are seeking in terms of high profitability and/or high turnover.

Source of value	Vision Goals
You ➢ Your role in the business ➢ Your creativity source skills, talents ➢ Your values: what is important to you?	
Customers ➢ Products/services ➢ Customer value: what benefits do you provide, what unmet needs do your products/services fulfil ➢ Customer base: geographical markets, business sectors ➢ Nature of customer relationships ➢ Corporate brand	

Source of value	Vision Goals
Your team ➤ Number of employees ➤ Organisational structure, skills ➤ Office, factory space ➤ Office culture: mindset, behaviours, values, atmosphere	
Processes and systems ➤ Logistics: delivery, distribution of products/services ➤ Physical assets required ➤ Efficient production of products/delivering services ➤ R&D new product/ service generation	
Time frame	
Financial : valuation, turnover, gross profit margin, net profit margin	

Chapter 15 : Where are you now?

Introduction

In working towards accomplishing the vision goals which you have identified in Chapter 14, you will also need to ascertain where you are now, in terms of how far you have already achieved the goals that you have set.

Where are you now?

The framework for your vision goals, on pages 55 and 56, can be extended by adding another column, 'where you are now' as shown on pages 58 and 59 and by introducing those factors which can provide sources of growth for your business. You can use this column to identify against each vision goal entry, where you are right at this moment in time with your business.

If you are currently in the process of starting up your business, you can complete the framework on pages 58 and 59 by using a combination of what you have accomplished so far, such as the skills and talents that you have, your brand values and culture and the products and services which you have available to offer to prospective customers.

Where you are already in business, then you will have actual data and results to include in the framework.

Source of value	Where you are now	Vision Goals
You ➢ Your role in the business ➢ Your creativity source, skills, talents ➢ Your values: what is important to you?		
Customers ➢ Products/services ➢ Customer value: what benefits do you provide, what unmet needs do you fulfil ➢ Customer base: geographical markets, business sectors ➢ Nature of customer relationships ➢ Corporate brand ➢ Identifying growth areas in your product lines/service streams ➢ Identifying growth areas in new markets and increasing customer base in existing markets ➢ Identifying other sources of growth such as joint ventures, franchising		

Source of value	Where you are now	Vision Goals
Your team ➢ Number of employees ➢ Organisational structure, skills ➢ Office, factory space ➢ Office culture: mindset, behaviours, values, atmosphere		
Processes and systems ➢ Logistics: delivery, distribution of products/services ➢ Physical assets required ➢ Efficient production of products/delivering services ➢ R&D new product/ service generation		
Time-frame		
Financial : valuation, turnover, gross profit margin, net profit margin		

Chapter 16 : Bridging the gap: growth phases

Introduction

The differences between where you want to be, with your vision goals and where you are now, represent the gaps that you need to bridge in order to progress forward and to ultimately arrive at your destination vision.

Bridging the gap – growth phases

In looking to work out how to bridge the gap between where you are now and where you want to be we use a combination of growth phases and sources of value (Chapter 17). The different growth phases act as stepping stones which connect you from where you are now to your vision.

The growth phases that we use in our framework are:

➢ **Start up phase:** creating a viable business which has a consistently positive cash flow and the foundations of a good quality customer base.

➢ **Momentum phase:** scaling up your business by building on your success in the start up phase.

➢ **Phenomenon phase:** a radical change in the rate of growth and development of your business.

➢ **Consolidating phase:** maintaining the success factors of your business and honing your business for a sale or preparing for others, such as family members or your management team to take over the business where you are looking to step back or retire.

The growth phases may differ for some businesses. For example, new or high technology firms may spend a longer period than other businesses in the start up growth phase as they create and perfect their products or services. However, the next phase, momentum growth, may be a very short time period especially where the technology allows for a rapidly scalable business, such as internet based technologies. Additionally, some business owners may choose from the outset to not go through the phenomenon growth phase, for example, where the vision is to create a business that is small enough to allow you to both continue to have a 'hands on' role and also to manage the rest of your business quite easily. Another, smaller business option could be a 'lifestyle' type business, that is a business of the size which provides for the annual income requirements of the owner and also surplus funds for perhaps investing elsewhere to provide for their long term wealth needs.

Additionally, where you are already in business you will need to identify which growth phase you are currently in. Where you identify two potential growth phases, such as start up and momentum phases, for example you have a good size client base but not yet a viable business in terms of its ongoing positive cash position, then you should look at which of the key challenges of the earlier growth phase have yet to be attained and to focus on completing these before moving on to the next growth phase.

An initial framework for identifying a growth plan for your business is shown on page 62. The framework would need to be adjusted for:

➢ Where you are now: If you are already active in your business then your starting point for where you are now would be the growth phase column which currently applies to your business.

➢ Smaller business size: If you are seeking to create a smaller size company that you wish to be involved in on a hands on basis, combining both producing and delivering your products and services as well as managing the business on a daily basis, then you would delete the phenomenon growth column.

	Where you are now	Start up growth	Momentum growth	Phenomenon growth	Consolidating phase	Vision goals
Key milestones for growth						
Time period for each growth phase						
Financial stretch goals for each phase						

Key milestones

The key milestones for growth are a summary of the key events in the development of your business. For example, if you envision creating a global business and you are currently looking to start up your business, then as an example, one of the key milestones could be expanding the geographical markets which you sell your products or deliver your services to. This could mean that in the start up phase you are looking to cover a local market, such as the particular city or county that is nearest to your business. The momentum phase could be creating a national network and the phenomenon growth phase could be securing a global presence. The consolidating phase could then involve a tidying up of your global market space, improving, refining and making your network more efficient and profitable. A good number of key milestones would be 3 to 5, as more than 5 can give you too many factors to keep focused on. Some examples of the key challenges which a business could well be facing in a particular growth phase and from which you can create those key milestones that are relevant for your business, include:

Start up growth phase

The overriding challenge in this first growth phase of a business is to create a viable business. A viable business is one that has a consistently positive cash flow, is able to pay you a level of remuneration on a consistent basis (albeit may be not quite at the level you set out in Chapter 8), has the foundations of a good quality customer base and provides some funds to reinvest in the future growth of your business. Some of the key challenges are:

➢ Identifying and refining your brand such as in formulating a compelling brand message which also reflects the values which are important to you.

➢ Creating and building up a quality customer base and identifying those key factors as to why your customers buy from you.

➢ Managing your time across the different job roles within a business whilst being able to consistently deliver on your brand promise.

➢ Managing your start up funds and generating a consistently positive cash-flow.

Momentum growth phase

The overriding objectives of this growth phase are to both maintain the success that you have created in the start up phase and to scale up your business as smoothly as possible so that you increase the speed of the growth, or the momentum, of your business. Some of the key challenges are:

➤ Further developing and refining your brand and communicating your brand message. Seeking feedback from your customers as to why they buy from you.

➤ Increasing your customer base whilst retaining the key clients won in the start up phase.

➤ Managing your time, delegating and training your team. Expanding, or even recruiting your first team.

➤ Developing efficient processes for your team to follow such as in sales generation, producing your goods, delivering services.

➤ Seeking feedback from your customers to identify their unmet needs for which you can add new products and service lines to your existing range.

Phenomenon growth phase

The overriding objectives of this growth phase are to both fund and implement a radical expansion in the size and scope of your business. Some of the key challenges are:

➤ Funding this significant expansionary phase.

➤ Planning your strategy for the rapid expansion of your business whilst at the same time continuing to serve the customer base that you have developed in the two earlier growth phases. Identifying new markets to sell your products and services into and also identifying new products and services for your rapidly expanding customer base.

➤ Realising the value in your brand in terms of finding out how strong your brand is in terms of how far you can extend your organisation. For example, you may be looking to develop a global reach in a particular business sector or you may be looking at operating in numerous unrelated business sectors but using the same corporate brand, such as the development of Sir Richard Branson's Virgin brand.

➤ Recruiting a professionally qualified senior management and board team. Embedding your required culture and behaviours in your new team whilst at the same time reviewing those cultural aspects from your new team members which you may wish to adopt in order to refine your existing organisational culture.

➤ Implementing efficient production and delivery processes with a significantly expanding organisation both in terms of the number of employees and the number of geographical locations which your business operates from.

➢ Implementing an efficient organisational structure which supports the culture of your business. For example, this could mean a head office structure which takes the key strategic decisions which are then passed down to the offices or business units to implement. Another structure could be to give the business units more control and autonomy over strategic decision making and implementation.

Consolidating growth phase

The overriding objectives of this 'consolidating' phase are firstly, to tidy up the rapid growth of the phenomenon growth phase and, where you are looking to step back from your business or to sell it, then a second aspect would be to ensure the smooth running of the business in your absence. Some of the key challenges are:

➢ Consolidating the value derived in the phenomenon growth phase such as in refining your brand to improve customer loyalty and often ongoing refinement in the differentiation of your products and services over those of your competitors.

➢ Changing your business growth strategy to one of lower rates of incremental growth, by for example, improving profitability through more efficient operations and incremental developments and extensions in your product and service portfolio.

➢ Ensuring your values and knowledge are embedded within your business so that the business does not lose value when you either step back from or leave the business.

➢ Preparing your business for sale.

Time period

The time period of each growth phase is specific to each business owner and their business, and is based on a number of factors, such as the ultimate size of business you wish to achieve with your vision, the speed of growth you wish to achieve and the overall time scale you have set for realising your vision.

For each growth phase, allocate a time period, such that the total of all of the time periods equals the overall time period that you have set for your vision. For example, if you are starting up your business now and you have a vision that you wish to accomplish within say 5 years, then the total of the time periods should be 5 years. The length of each time period is your choice, and there is no particular reason to assume that each growth phase should be of the same duration as the other phases. For example, a 5 year vision may have a start up phase of 6 months, that is the 6 months from the date that you start your business; a momentum phase of 6 to 18 months; a phenomenon growth phase of 18 to 48 months and a consolidating phase of 48 to 60 months, that is from years 4 to 5. The time periods which you select are your choice – there is no rulebook as to how fast businesses grow and ultimately the rate of growth is determined by you and your team, such as how focused you are, how persistent and resilient you are and how inspired and motivated you are to accomplish the big vision that you have set.

Financial stretch goals

With financial goal setting, first you need to be clear on which financial measure or measures you are looking for your business to achieve. For example, are you looking at a turnover target or a net profit before tax target or another financial measure? Your financial goals should also take into account both your annual income requirements from your business and also your long term financial goal.

Allocate a financial goal for your business to accomplish by the end of each growth phase. For example, keeping with our 5 year vision in the example above and if we wanted to create a business with £20 million turnover, we might select financial goals for the start up phase of £200,000, a momentum phase of £1.5 million, a phenomenon growth phase of £15 million and a consolidating phase of £20 million.

The stretch goal refers to the range of your financial goals for each growth phase, which is to stretch from the end of the previous growth phase to the target you wish to achieve by the end of the current growth phase. So for example, in the scenario in the above paragraph, the stretch goal for the momentum growth phase would be to increase your turnover from £200,000 at the start of the growth phase to £1,500,000 by the end of the growth phase. In estimating your financial goals you should assume that your financial results will grow exponentially rather than linearly, increasing at a rapid rate in the early years of your business and then significantly more slowly when your business is in the consolidating growth phase.

Again, there is no rule book on the numbers to select here. Businesses grow at different rates depending on the vision set out for them, the actions and mindset of the business owner, the business sector that you operate in and the speed at which your business allows you to scale up its size. For example an internet based business can often be scaled up much more rapidly than one that has more employees, more physical fixed assets such as buildings and machinery and production or service delivery requirements.

Moving from one growth phase to another

Transitioning from one growth phase to another can present businesses with a number of challenges rather than being a naturally smooth process.

Working on and accomplishing any particular growth phase usually involves a significant amount of time, energy and effort from everyone involved in helping to grow your business and in the early days can also involve a measure of sacrifice in terms of financial reward. Accomplishing all or most of the goals that you set out for a particular growth phase is a time for much celebration of the success you have achieved.

The transition phase acts like a plateau, a leveling off in activity as you not only celebrate your achievements but also you take time to reflect on and consolidate all that has happened in the seeming whirlwind of growth activity. This could include catching up with any outstanding documentation, such as updating the customer relationship management systems (CRM) that you use and any accounting documentation, whether internally or externally for your accountant. Also taking the time and space to understand what has worked particularly well with your brand and culture, your systems, identifying and responding to customer needs to further improve the quality of your products and services and identifying sources of future innovations. In addition, it is a time for looking outwards to see what is going on externally which could impact your business right now and potentially in the future, such as changes in the composition of your competitors, changes in their product and service offerings, changes in the structure of your 'industry' or business sector and changes in the wider global environment.

After this feedback and analysis phase, and where further growth is sought then there is the need to map out the plan for the next growth phase. For example, do you need to update the growth phase plan, identified originally, for those target goals which you have exceeded? Perhaps you have identified new growth opportunities which have arisen during the growth phase just accomplished. Thereafter it is a case of gearing yourself up to kick start the next growth phase and also to inspire and motivate those around you who you wish to take part in the next stage of your adventure. In starting a new growth phase you may be required to engender a sense of urgency within both yourself and your team to be able to work at the pace you require in order to be able to achieve the next growth phase within the time-scale that you have set out.

Starting another growth phase again requires much energy and stamina and an ability to willingly and actively cope with an even more intense working life than in the previous phase. It is to be noted that not everyone may share your energy, stamina and enthusiasm, in particular those who are not used to a rapidly changing organisation as the 'norm' for a work environment. Some people are used to one big push to work to create significant change within an organisation and thereafter seek to return to their default comfort zone. There can be the very reasonable belief that there is no urgent need to change again, since the business is on a sound footing and that there seems to be no immediate danger to them either losing their job or in their employer's ability to pay their wages over the foreseeable future. In such cases it can be difficult to create the sense of urgency required to both kick start and to maintain a high state of focused activity as you try to take your business through another rapid and significant growth phase.

A period of transition between two growth phases can be particularly tricky in that you are putting your business into a state of flux, from which the outcomes can include the successful achievement of the next growth phase, or an ongoing plateau with your business seeming to rigidly stick at the same size, or even going backwards and losing the gains and momentum that you and your team have worked so hard to achieve. The sticking or reversal scenarios can arise for various reasons, such as:

➤ You, as the business owner are not fully committed to the next growth phase, or further growth generally. For example, you may have achieved your own particular financial goals, such as the annual income figure identified in Chapter 8; fears about stepping into the unknown, uncharted territory if, for example, you have not been involved at a senior level of a business of the size that you seek to realise in the next growth phase.

➤ Failure to provide strong leadership to your team so that they do not actively work with you to move your business in the direction in which you wish to take it.

➤ Not building strong systems and business processes as your business grows, so that you can free up your time and gradually step back from having a hands on role within your business to a role which is predominantly focused on leadership.

- Not developing a loyal customer following through strong, trusted and committed relationships with your key customers.

- Lack of financial controls and timely financial reporting with which to understand, monitor and analyse your business.

- Lack of a strong team such as retaining a core of employees who are able to grow and develop their skills as your business grows or in identifying which key skills that you need in your team, and by when do you need them to be working in your business and additionally in being able to attract skilled individuals to your team.

- Complacency in your organisation's regard for your customers such as not continually seeking to provide good value in the benefits and service provided. A complacent organisation can often stop listening to customers for their feedback and thus miss vital information on new product and service opportunities which contribute to further growth in your business.

- Over-confidence within your organisation in terms of thinking that your business is immune to competitors, to changes in your industry or to changes in the economy generally and that your customers wouldn't dream of going elsewhere.

Chapter 17 : Sources of Value

Introduction

The sources of value help you to build in the detail as to how you are going to accomplish the key milestones which you have set for each growth phase that you have identified for your business. The sources of value also connect the growth phases back to the vision goals and the 'where you are now' sections in Chapters 14 and 15, respectively.

Sources of value are common to all businesses and in all business sectors and also common to whatever the size of your business or the growth phase that it is in. The unique entity that is your business is derived from your own personal interpretation of each source and in how you combine the sources to work together. The sources of value used in this handbook are:

➢ You, as the business owner.

➢ Your customers.

➢ Your team.

➢ Your business processes and systems.

➢ Planning your business including financial planning.

How you interpret and combine the sources of value help you to create your unique business and also help you to define how you set your business apart from your competitors. Each of the sources of value develops as you take your business through each growth phase. The frameworks below show examples of the development of each source as a business grows and becomes more complex in its structure. You can use the frameworks as guides to identify how you seek to develop your business as you take it from where you are now to where you wish to arrive with your long term vision.

Additionally, within each growth phase you will identify your unique mix or combination of the different sources of value which seek to achieve the key milestones which you have set. Part 4 provides you with tools to help you to fine-tune the combinations and to help you to develop a variety of options from which you can work out how to achieve the financial targets identified for each growth phase as well as helping you to identify areas of flexibility within your business model.

You, as the business owner

Over the lifetime of your business, your role should change from, at the start of your business, of probably performing most of the tasks to ultimately, when you sell or retire from your business, having a role such that your business is able to function well and efficiently in your absence.

	Examples of your changing role
Stat up growth phase	➢ Undertaking most of the job roles where funds limit you from taking on employees ➢ Allocating your time between promoting your business, running the business and doing the work that you are most talented at doing ➢ Identifying your brand values and what is important to you to communicate and deliver in what you produce and sell and how you deliver your service ➢ Identifying your organisation's cultural values
Momentum growth phase	➢ Training your team, delegating tasks and trusting your new team to complete the tasks that you set ➢ Managing your team, reviewing work and providing feedback ➢ Communicating and transferring your skills and talents to your team ➢ Recruiting to your team those members who are talented at those skills that are not your strong points, so that you develop a strong and balanced business
Phenomenon growth phase	➢ Stepping back from the day to day management of your business ➢ Delegating leadership responsibilities to your key members of staff ➢ Predominantly working at a high level within your business and charting your course to your vision
Consolidating growth phase	➢ Stepping into a smaller role or leaving the business to pursue other ventures or interests ➢ Your business should now be running well independently of you ➢ Preparing your replacements to easily step into your role when you depart via a programme of mentoring and training to fully transfer your values, your culture, your brand and skills and expertise

Your customers

Over the lifetime of your business you are looking to create a loyal and profitable customer base, to extend your products and services and the markets you serve as far as you are able or as far as is required to meet your financial targets. In addition, there will also be continuous development and refinement of your value proposition, that is, the combination of your brand (what you provide and how you provide it) and your pricing, in order to enable you to capture as much value, in terms of achieving your financial targets.

	Your customers
Stat up growth phase	➢ Identifying your initial range of products/services ➢ Clarifying and refining your value proposition: successfully communicating your brand, the price or fee that you charge and the benefits you offer to your potential customers ➢ Identifying which initial 'segment' of potential customers to focus your sales and promotional drive on ➢ Deciding on your promotional activities e.g. one to one networking, group seminars, presentations, telemarketing, advertising, the internet
Momentum growth phase	➢ Further developing your value proposition: successfully communicating your brand, the price or fee that you charge, the benefits or opportunities that you offer your potential customers ➢ Expanding your customer base, increasing customer profitability, retention of quality customers, increasing their expenditure with your business ➢ Introducing new products and/or services ➢ Expanding into new customer niches or markets
Phenomenon growth phase	➢ Radically expanding your customer base, possibly by developing a global customer base ➢ Moving into new product and service markets which complement the markets you are already in ➢ Potentially acquiring competitors ➢ Moving up or down or changing the 'chain' of your industry. For example a business acquires a distributor for their products or sells over the internet direct to the end user customer and cutting out the distributor ➢ Developing a brand portfolio where you offer a range of different products and/or services
Consolidating growth phase	➢ Consolidating your customer base, focusing on profitability and retention ➢ Moving into new product and service markets which complement the markets you are already in ➢ Incremental developments in and extensions to your product and service portfolio ➢ Developing a brand portfolio where you offer a range of different products and services

Your team

In creating and developing your team over the course of the growth of your business you are chiefly looking to embed the right type of culture within your expanding team and also creating a strong and dynamic team which can increasingly and ultimately run your business well and efficiently in your absence.

	Your team
Stat up growth phase	➢ Finding and recruiting employees; training, delegation, reviewing work done ➢ Identifying which non-core activities to outsource ➢ Finding your team of advisors e.g. accountant, lawyer, mentor, coach ➢ Building your network of contacts
Momentum growth phase	➢ Finding and recruiting employees; training, delegation, reviewing work done ➢ Communicating and instilling the culture of your business to your new team members ➢ Motivating and inspiring your team and providing a career path for those who you wish to retain in your business
Phenomenon growth phase	➢ Recruiting professionally qualified senior management and board of directors ➢ Giving high level decision making responsibilities to your senior managers and directors ➢ Deciding on the organisational and reporting structures for the many employees now working in your organisation ➢ Dealing with the major challenge of maintaining the strong culture which you have developed to date whilst at the same time incorporating the positive elements brought by your senior management team and board
Consolidating growth phase	➢ Professionally qualified senior management and board of directors having high level decision making responsibilities ➢ Embedding and maintaining a dynamic, creative and entrepreneurial culture ➢ Having a team which can run your business in your absence as well as dealing with strategic decision making and leadership of your organisation

Processes and systems

When you start your business you should be looking to create formal processes and systems of the way you carry out the various different job roles so that these can be easily passed on to new members of your team, who in turn can take on the training role. Additionally, you are looking to produce and deliver your products and services as efficiently as possible in order to not dilute the profits and profitability of your business.

	Processes and systems
Stat up growth phase	<ul><li>Allocating your time between delivering your products and services, finding new customers and developing ongoing business relationships with your valued customers</li><li>Creating a system for converting sales leads into orders and contracts</li><li>Identifying and implementing an efficient process for the creation and delivery of each product or service that you offer</li><li>Ensuring you get paid on time in accordance with your terms and conditions of business</li></ul>
Momentum growth phase	<ul><li>Set performance targets for your team, reviewing progress and providing timely feedback and rewarding performance</li><li>Implementing processes and procedures for your team to follow</li><li>Identifying and implementing an efficient process for the creation and delivery of each product or service that you offer</li><li>Team working and inter-departmental communication between your team</li><li>Moving to larger premises</li></ul>
Phenomenon growth phase	<ul><li>Identifying acquisition targets and estimating the value that you can extract post-acquisition</li><li>Reviewing high level performance measures, for example comparing performance between multiple sites of operation</li><li>Global supply chain logistics</li><li>Highly formalised working procedures and processes and staff appraisal systems</li><li>Moving to larger or multi-site premises and perhaps in different countries</li></ul>
Consolidating growth phase	<ul><li>Reviewing high level performance measures, for example comparing performance between multiple sites of operation</li><li>Global supply chain logistics</li><li>Highly formalised working procedures and processes and staff appraisal systems</li></ul>

Planning

Planning covers many aspects including financial and organisational planning, reviewing and analysing current results. There is also planning for the future development of your business in terms of charting the path to your vision as well as finding ways to reduce the downside risks in the decisions you take.

	Planning
Stat up growth phase	➢ Securing initial funds to set up your business and to provide initial working capital funds ➢ Cash flow forecasting and working capital management so that the minimum amount of cash is tied up within your business. Ensuring monthly cash flows cover your business expenses and provide you with what you determine to be a reasonable or required level of remuneration ➢ Reviewing and analysing monthly management reports from your accounting software ➢ Comparing your actual results with those forecast in your financial goals ➢ Reviewing the effectiveness of your sales and promotional activities ➢ Formally setting out your terms and conditions of business with your customers
Momentum growth phase	➢ Increasing profitability ➢ Cash flow forecasting and working capital management ➢ Reviewing and analysing monthly management reports. Comparing your results with those forecast in your stretch financial goals ➢ Reviewing the effectiveness of your sales and promotional activities, what conversion rates does your sales funnel reveal? ➢ Expanding your office and production space and increasing fixed asset expenditure such as IT systems and assets used to produce your products or to deliver your services ➢ Retaining funds to help finance the next growth phase
Phenomenon growth phase	➢ Acquisition strategy if expansion is wholly or partly from acquiring other businesses. Fast growth markets after a period of time can often go through a shake out phase where the stronger players acquire their competitors to confirm their position in their market as a key player with significant market share ➢ Securing funds for growth and exploring the variety of financial tools available to structure your funding requirements ➢ Efficiency in multiple sites of operation
Consolidating growth phase	➢ Planning for a lower growth phase ➢ Integrating previous acquisitions into your business, such as dealing with differences in the corporate culture, merging IT systems and data, retaining key staff in the acquired businesses, ensuring the value expected to be derived from the acquisition translates into actual results, reconfiguring organisational structures and site locations ➢ Multiple sites of operation ➢ Preparing for the sale of your business or your stepping back to a smaller role

Summary

Part 3 has been concerned with connecting your long term vision to the here and now. Our framework comprises the following elements:

➢ Setting the long term vision goals for your business whereby when you have achieved these specific and measurable goals you have realised your business vision.

➢ Identifying where you are now in terms of reaching your vision goals.

➢ Between the boundaries of where you are now and your vision is a gap. Seeking to bridge the gap with using the various growth phases which you wish to take your business through.

➢ Each growth phase has a number of key milestones which set out in summary what you want to achieve in terms of how you see your business developing, with each growth phase building on the success of the previous phase. For each growth phase you have estimated both a time frame to achieve the milestones and a number of financial targets.

➢ The detail as to how you achieve the key milestones is provided by your interpretation and combination of the sources of value, out of which you create your unique business.

The time period and financial targets provide you with goals to aim for. You may reach the targets in a quicker time frame or even a longer time frame than you have estimated. You do not know what you are capable of realising and accomplishing until you start on your journey. Identifying measurable targets provides you with specifics to focus on, without which you could easily fall foul of the adage 'failing to plan is planning to fail'.

The framework which we introduced on pages 55 and 56 has been developed throughout Part 3 and a summary of our expanded framework is set out on pages 77 and 78.

	Where you are now	Start up growth phase	Momentum growth phase	Phenomenon growth phase	Consolidating growth phase	Vision goals
Key Milestones						
You						
Customers						
Your team						

	Where you are now	Start up growth phase	Momentum growth phase	Phenomenon growth phase	Consolidating growth phase	Vision goals
Processes and Systems						
Planning						
Time-frame						
Financial goals						

PART 4 – FINE-TUNING YOUR BUSINESS MODEL

Chapter 18 : Business Model

Introduction

Part 4 is concerned with fine-tuning how you seek to achieve the financial and growth goals for your business. In this section we look at honing your business model and the following applies to each of the growth phases which you choose to implement for your business.

A business model is simply how your business makes money, and in this handbook, making money whilst building a business around your talents and at the same time working towards achieving a long term vision which you are truly passionate about bringing into reality.

The following chapters provide further detail on the following 3 variables which were introduced in Chapter 13:

➢ Cash.

➢ Profits.

➢ Growth.

These variables often require constant review and continuous attention as you seek to develop and grow your business. Your business needs inflows of cash to continue as a viable business. Your business needs to be profitable to remain viable over the short and medium term and also to continually seek out growth opportunities in order to achieve the long term size and value targets that you have set. All 3 elements are required to develop a strong and sustainable business.

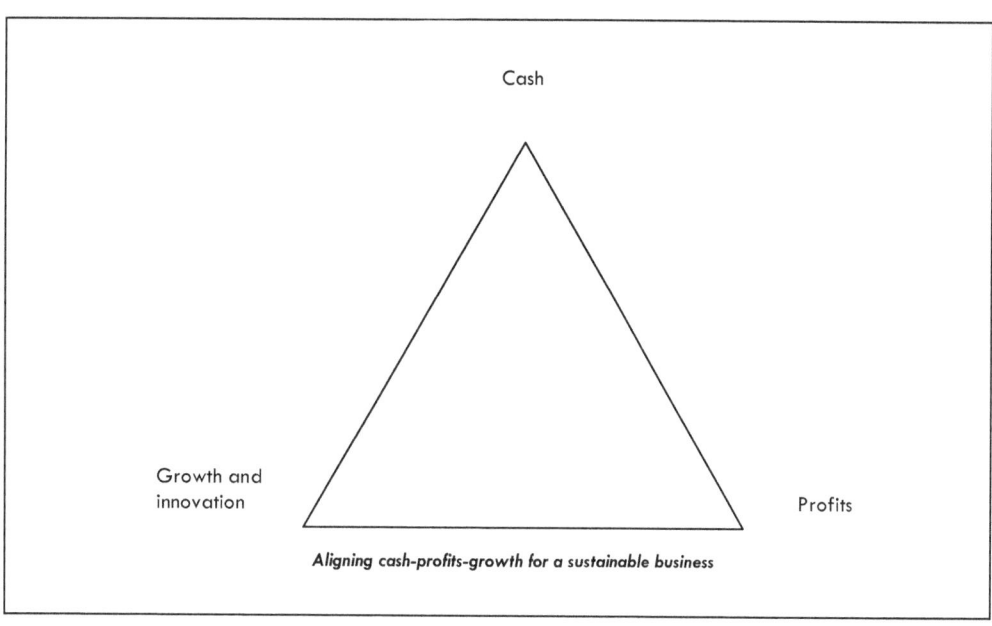

Aligning cash-profits-growth for a sustainable business

Chapter 19 : Cash

Introduction

The immediate viability concerns of your business are determined by your cash balances and cash flows, such that if you run out of cash then your business can cease very quickly without an injection of funds to cover the shortfall. Without a good understanding of how your business generates and uses cash, that is the stock of cash (the balance in your business bank account) and the flows – in their timing and magnitude - you can never really be sure of the viability let alone the strength and sustainability of your business over the longer term.

Cash balances

Cash balances are simply the total amount in your business bank accounts at any point in time. Cash balances are influenced by the net difference between cash inflows (such as receipts from customers) and cash outflows (such as expenditure on purchases, employee wages and salaries). Over time, where accumulated cash inflows exceed cash outflows then your cash balances will increase. Other cash flows include sources of funding such as the initial cash you use to start the business where this comes from your own personal funds; funding from external shareholder investors; bank and other sources of loan funding. The stock of cash on an ongoing basis is affected by:

➢ The price you charge for your products and services.

➢ Any discounts you give to your customers.

➢ The amount of time it takes to collect amounts due from your customers in respect of the goods and services that they have bought from you.

Having a business model which seeks to build up cash balances allows for the immediate survival of your business as you should have the cash funds to meet ongoing expenses and also to meet larger annual lumps of expenditure, such as the company tax liability.

Having funds which exceed your annual ongoing expenses also helps you to build your business and to take it to its next level of development by being able to re-invest funds in the next phase of capital or growth related expenditure, such as buying larger premises.

Having cash balances in excess of your immediate requirements gives your business a cash buffer which can help you to cope with unforeseen circumstances, such as the loss of a large customer or suffering a large bad debt or perhaps a competitor instigates a price cutting policy to win market share and to take some of your customers.

Cash flows

Cash-flow is the life blood of the business. If cash inflows are less than you require in order to meet your expenditure, you will have a negative cash flow and if this continues over time your business can fold. The key elements of cash flow management include knowing the amount of cash coming in to your business, understanding the timing of these inflows as well as the amount and timing of cash flows going out of your business. It is vital to have a good understanding of the amounts and timing of both cash inflows and cash outflows both currently and in the future.

The main tool for getting to grips with the cash flow 'pulse' of your business is a cash flow forecast. Cash flow forecasts are usually prepared on a monthly basis – showing the amount of cash receipts you expect to receive in a given month and deducting your expected payments. The monthly calculations are also usually cumulated to prepare an annual cash-flow forecast. These initial calculations are based on your expectations and assumptions. These calculations should then be reviewed each month and compared against actual results.

Cash flow forecasts are also used to see the effects of trying out different scenarios, such as the effect of introducing changes to the terms of trade you offer to customers or in changes that are instigated by your customers, such as an increase in the average time they take to pay you. Trying out different scenarios, or 'what if' analyses can help you to see the potential longer term effect of changes, and in particular identify those changes which work favourably for your business in terms of improving your cash position or unfavourably in terms of worsening your cash position and potentially giving you a shortfall in cash. Projecting your cash position into the future allows you to identify shortages in advance. Having as much advance warning as possible of your forthcoming projected cash position gives you more time to formulate and implement an action plan to fill the cash-gap, by for example, working with your customers to reduce the time it takes to collect your debts, to reduce or delay forthcoming expenditure or to use one of the many external means of financing, such as bank overdrafts, lending, introducing your own personal funds, and factoring working capital balances. Having less or no time to plan for cash shortfalls reduces, and can even remove, the number of options available to you.

A simplified example of the working capital 'system' of a business is shown below (on page 85). In this example, receiving an order from a customer produces a flow of activity to produce a product or to deliver a service. When the product/service is delivered an invoice is raised for the sale. The invoice is on credit terms, such as a 30 day payment period. All being well, the business receives the payment 30 days after issuing the invoice. The payment is then added to the bank account, and increases the cash balance. The cash may then be retained in the bank account, paid out to buy more of the items that help you to produce and or deliver your product or service such as, buying materials and paying yourself and your employees. Alternatively, the cash may be used on other non-working capital expenditure such as paying taxes and overhead costs, such as utility bills.

Identifying the working capital system which applies to your business can help you to identify any gaps or blockages by working your way through each item and flow in the 'system'. In addition, where you implement changes or improvements in your working capital system you can estimate the effects on your cash balances and cash-flows by using cash-flow forecasts. For example, a review of your working capital system could identify:

➢ Delays in transferring a customer order to someone responsible for production and/or delivery. A manual transfer system can have production and delivery delays which can be easily and quickly reduced.

➢ Delays in producing an invoice for a customer after the delivery of the product or service.

➢ Delays in the time taken by customers to pay you in respect of credit sales which exceed the time stated in your terms of trade. You can see from a 'what-if' calculation the effect that such delays have in worsening your cash position. Being able to see the numerical effect can often help to ensure that you and your team encourage your customers to adhere to your stated terms of trade.

➢ Consider changes in the time-scale within which customers pay you. For example, if your terms of trade are 30 days, is there a particular reason for this? What scope is there for changing, say a 30 day period to 14 days or less and to zero days where payment is required before delivery.

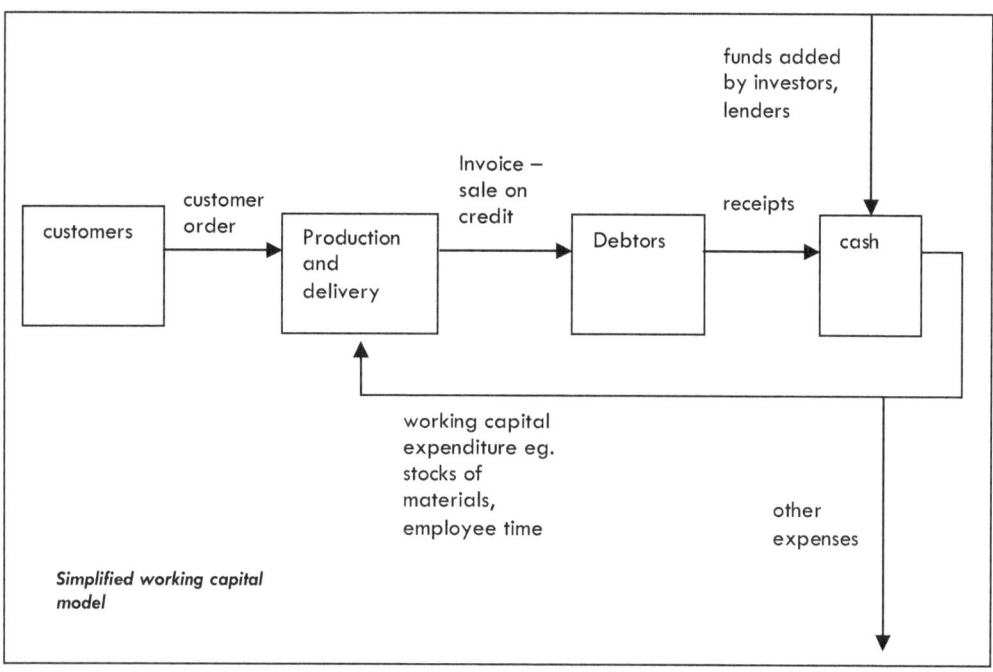

Simplified working capital model

- Cash-flow forecasts and what-if calculations can provide you with hard data as to the size of the negative impact on your cash flows from giving discounts.

- A what-if analysis can also show you different scenarios from changing the time-scale in which you pay your expenditure, for example in amounts you owe to suppliers or in deferring larger items of expenditure.

- Working your way through your working capital system can also highlight other delays such as customer queries received over incomplete deliveries or queries over the correct pricing and discounting of items. All of which lengthen the time it takes for your business to be paid for the products it has delivered and the cost of which you are likely to have to fund from sources other than the customer who owes you money.

Chapter 20 : Profits

Introduction

The profits of a business take on a more short and medium term time frame, compared with the immediate importance and viability attaching to the cash that your business generates. The profits are the paper flows, arising from the difference between sales invoices generated and purchase invoices received together with non-cash or accounting adjustments such as depreciation for a particular time period. For example, the time period would be each month for preparing monthly management accounts and usually a year for preparing the accounts for a business.

Simplified profits model

A simplified profits model is shown below on page 87. Each product line and service stream contributes to the turnover that your business generates. The model below shows a business with 3 products and services. Your turnover model may be more complicated, for example where you charge different prices for the same product or service or you have many more individual products and services. The profits of a business are then calculated by deducting costs from the total turnover generated. The profits figure can be calculated for any time period you choose, usually for a month where you are preparing management accounts and annually when preparing your year end accounts. The profits figure shown below would be the net profit before tax figure in your year end accounts. Costs would include those costs or expenses which related to the period for which you are preparing the accounts, and will often include invoiced amounts and accounting adjustments, such as for any stocks and depreciation.

The simplified profits model shows that you have a number of variables to 'play' with in terms of how to calculate how to reach the financial goals which you have set for your business for a particular growth phase, for example:

➢ The variety of turnover targets which can be achieved using different quantity combinations for each product and service

➢ Seeing the effect on your profits figure from making changes in a price for one or any combination of your products and services. Even a small increase in price can have a significant effect on your profits.

➢ How different cost estimates impact on both the absolute profits figure and in the rate of profit margin derived by your business.

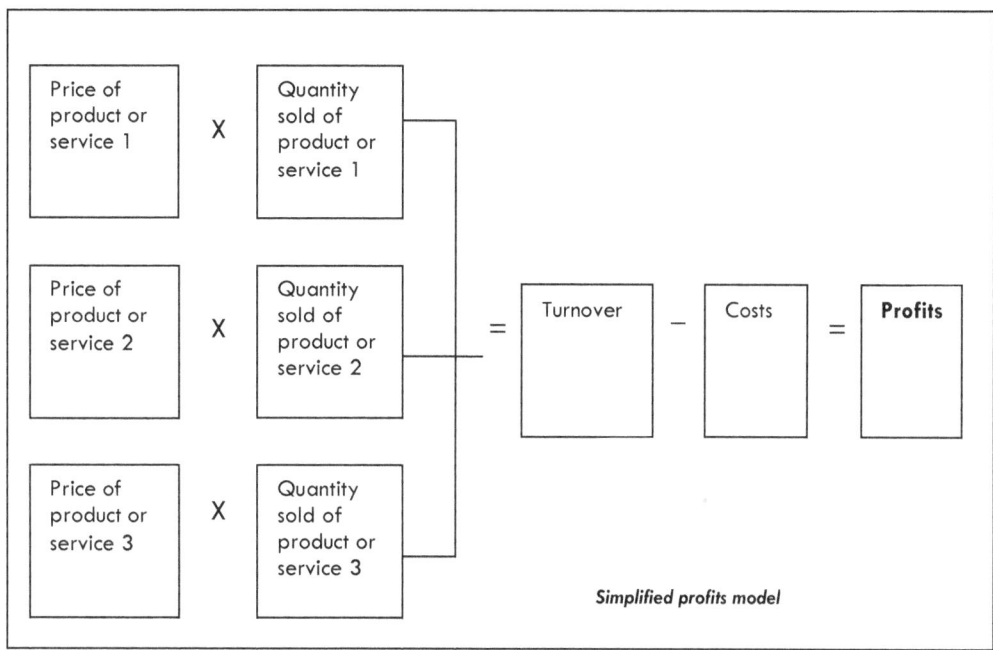

Simplified profits model

Turnover

The turnover of a business is affected by the prices you charge, the discounts you give to your customers and the quantity of goods or services sold. Your customer base at any point in time comprises new customers making their first purchase with you (converted from prospects by your sales team) and existing customers making repeat purchases. The impact on turnover of repeat customers is in both the frequency by which a customer purchases from you and in the amount that they spend in each purchase. Increasing the frequency of purchase can come from building long term relationships with your customers as well as having a pro-active sales team. The amount a customer spends with your business is affected by the number of repeat purchases of the same product/service as well as providing additional products or services that they wish to buy.

Pricing

The pricing of your products and services is often the most important factor in the profits and profitability of your business. A 1992 survey by management consultants, McKinsey, of 2,483 companies found that a 1% increase in price improves operating profit by 11.1%, compared with a 1% improvement in fixed costs producing a 2.3% improvement in profit, a 1% improvement in quantity sold improved profits by 3.3% and a 1% improvement in variable costs improved profit by 7.8%. Therefore, a small change in price can dramatically affect your profits.

'Pricing is the worst managed of all marketing areas. How prices are decided is often a mixture of voodoo and bingo' (Mark Ritson). Pricing can be a particularly tricky area, with different business departments involved in deriving the price charged for a product or service, such as the finance department and the marketing department, and who use different bases for arriving at their chosen price. For example, a finance department type approach would often involve deriving a price based on the costs of making the product/delivering the service such as a mark-up on cost or a profit margin. The marketing department may well use a basis of 'value', such as the value or benefit received by a customer, or group of customers with similar needs. Another element of the difficulty with pricing is the emotional attachment to an existing price and a mindset along the lines of, 'if we increase the price then customers will stop buying from us and go to a competitor'. Where this fear of increasing a price is in the mind of the business owner, then the pricing challenge becomes even more tricky.

There is unlikely to be one 'correct' price since each customer will have their own ideas and perceptions as to what price they would be prepared to pay for your product or service before seeking out an alternative – either going to one of your competitors or finding a different solution to the 'problem' that they are currently using your product or service to solve.

Where customers have difficulty distinguishing your products and services from those offered by your competitors then you have less scope for varying your price from that charged by your competitors. Taken to the extreme where your product or service is being regarded as a 'commodity' by customers then these items tend to be bought at the lowest possible price which a buyer can find.

In the absence of a perceived commodity status, there will often be a range of prices over which any particular customer would be happy to pay for your product or service before starting to shop around for a cheaper price. This is because customers use their own particular combination of reasons as to why they buy from you rather than a competitor. Additionally, the importance of each reason or decision buying factor often varies from customer to customer. The decision buying factors can be many and varied but often include 'perceived product benefits' such as price, flexibility, speed of delivery, dependability (receiving the right products and services and receiving them by the due delivery date) and quality. As well as their perceived product benefits, each customer will also have their own 'perceived emotional associations' attaching to the products and services they buy from you and also emotional perceptions as to how you and your team interact or deal with them. "Value can be defined as a combination of a set of product benefits plus emotional associations at an identified price level" (Cram).

This handbook looks at the pricing challenge from the perspective of finding a price which seeks to capture as much 'value' as customers perceive your product/service to be worth, rather than a cost-based price. The reason for this is that your customers buy from you based on their perceptions of value. Additionally, each business is unique and where customers understand and find benefit in the unique aspects of what your business produces and in how it is delivered then you have more scope to be rewarded for your uniqueness in the prices that you charge. A win-win outcome arises with happy and loyal customers and a strong and healthy business for you.

"Success comes from offering specific customers a clear combination of benefit and price that they will find attractive. A statement summarising this targeted offer is called a 'value proposition'." (Cram):

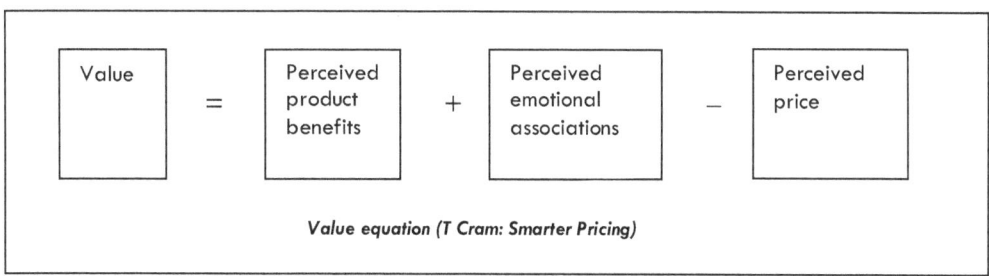

Value equation (T Cram: Smarter Pricing)

"Brands create value for customers by developing products and services that customers need, and surrounding them with positive association" (Cram).

Communicating your value proposition for each of your products and services through your sales and marketing work – the messages and manner of delivery by your sales team, in your advertising and promotional materials and in your internet presence, is a continual exercise in composing, measuring the response and refining what and how you communicate your message. It involves being clear on your brand values and understanding how your values and messages are being received by your prospective and existing customers, for example, do they understand your message and is it compelling enough to persuade them to buy your products and services the first time and then repeatedly once they have experienced the benefits provided by your products and services?

It is important to understand and to continually review the value that your customers receive from using your products and services. One way to do this is by using customer questionnaires which seek feedback on the different elements of service that you provide as well as ascertaining the importance of each element of service received. The latter collation and analysis of information allows you to understand what is important to your customers, some of which will have the same or similar value 'need's' and which you can group together to form groups or segments of customers and work out which of these groups are the more profitable key customer groups. Analysis of customer feedback should also include a comparison of how your products and services compare to those of your competitors and identifying the elements which are important to your customers and which you should exceed your competitors at providing. The elements or buying decision factors which are important to your customers may well also be important to the customers of your competitors and hence a good area on which to seek to attract your competitor's customers. The feedback can also give you information on how to market your products and services to new customers who are not yet using your or your competitor's products and services.

Efficiency

Efficiency is concerned with 'doing more with less' with any particular system within your business. More can include producing more goods and services with the same or less assets, such as machinery, office space, and the time of your team. Having formal systems and processes can help you to see where you can become more efficient and also to quickly see what is working well and what isn't and thus where you can make improvements in how you do things. Where you have a formal system you can check its efficiency – in particular whether you can identify any gaps or blockages in the system – by checking each stage of the process and the ease, or otherwise in which items, such as the production and delivery of a product or service or documentation, flows or passes from one part of the system to the next. You can also look at the system as a whole, for example, if you were to start with a blank sheet of paper would you construct the process differently in order to achieve a better result?

The utilisation of your key income producing assets impacts on your profitability. It can be fairly straightforward to measure the efficiency of a piece of equipment but often less so where your key assets are your employees (unless you have some form of time recording system). The aim is to find the balance between a good rate of utilisation which does not regularly push assets or people into over-capacity i.e. having too much work to do in the time available.

Another area to consider is in the way your business utilises its high cost 'assets', such as people and in particular, matching the quality of work to the most appropriate skill level of each person in your team. For example, with high cost employees are they doing as far as possible the work that they are most skilled at doing or are there aspects of their work which can be delegated to less senior team members, who are able to provide the same quality of output but at a cheaper cost, whilst at the same time freeing up time of high cost members who are then able to produce more of the products and services that you recruited them to do.

Costs

The absolute size of your costs affects the level of profits and profitability of your company. The lower are your costs then the higher are your profits. The type of cost is also relevant, whether the expense is a variable cost or a fixed cost. A variable cost is one that varies with the level of production or service delivery. For example, if you sub-contract part of your production, such as sub-contract labour then you would only incur the cost of the labour should you have an order in place and incur no expense where you have no order. A fixed cost, such as an employee's salary, is one that you have to pay whether or not you have an order to produce or a contract to deliver.

In the early days of a new business there is likely to be more focus on increasing the proportion of variable costs to fixed costs as there are fewer customer orders which can mean that a fixed cost item, such as a full time employee or piece of equipment is sitting around 'idle' for a good amount of time. It is usually cheaper to use sub-contract manpower and to hire equipment. As a business takes on more orders it often becomes cheaper to have fixed cost items where the cost allocated over the capacity usage is lower than the variable cost. Additionally over time, where you have ironed out the glitches in your business systems, you may find that out-sourcing a system may prove more cost-effective than continuing to keep it in-house.

Customer profitability

A further enhancement of the simplified profits model above is to calculate the profit of each customer, especially your key customers. Your key customers are those who contribute the majority of your turnover and/or profits. A common rule of thumb is that approximately 20% of your customers contribute 80% of your turnover or profits. The remaining 80% of your customers may provide a relatively small amount of profit, no profit or even a loss.

It can be somewhat less than straightforward to calculate the profit contributed by each customer. The simpler costs to identify, within a well structured accounting system, are ascertaining the direct costs incurred by each customer, such as the cost of materials used in producing the goods that they have bought and the time of your employees where you use a system of time sheets to record which clients an individual has worked on together with the amount of time that they have worked. Other less easy to identify costs, but no less important include the time taken to deal with the customer and to manage the customer relationship, for example additional time to deal with a complicated order, a problem with the delivery of a product, customer queries and complaints and resolving these as well as the amount of time taken to chase for payment.

Where you identify non-profit contributing customers it is your decision, as business owner to decide whether to keep that customer, and if so whether you wish to seek to improve the profitability. Some loss making customers you naturally wish to keep, perhaps because they refer other customers to you or are likely to provide your business with increased turnover and profitability in the foreseeable future, and at the moment you are making an investment in the relationship. Retaining difficult customers can be a drain on both your profitability and the morale of your team.

Customer retention

"It has been suggested that it costs up to five times as much to win a new customer as it does to retain an existing customer". (McDonald and Christopher)

"Bain and Company has suggested that even a relatively small improvement in the customer retention rate (measured as the percentage of retained business from one period to another) can have a marked impact on profitability. Their research indicates that, on average, an improvement of 5% in customer retention can lead to profit improvements of between 25% and 95% in the net present value of the future flow of earnings, depending on the industry" (McDonald and Christopher). Some of the reasons noted for the positive impact on profitability are the increased purchases by the customer; reduced operating costs since a business does not incur the costs of winning a new customer to make the same sale to; referrals provided by the existing customer; and charging a price premium since loyal customers are often less price sensitive and less inclined to change suppliers because of a price rise.

In addition, research into customer retention rates also shows that the higher the customer retention rate then the longer the period over which a customer remains with your business. "There is a direct linkage between the customer retention rate and the average duration of a customer relationship. For example, if the customer retention rate is 90% per annum (meaning that 10% of the existing customer base is lost each year) then the average customer lifetime will be 10 years" (Reichheld and Sasser research for Bain and Company).

Chapter 21 : Growth

Introduction

In order to achieve the long term business size and financial targets which you have set as part of your vision for your business you will often need to be both creative in seeking ways to grow your business as well as very active in seeking out new growth opportunities. Growth can be organic, with ideas, new products and services being created and developed internally from within the business. Growth, especially rapid growth can also come from external sources, such as from acquiring another business or in partnering with other businesses. Additionally, growth can come from incremental improvements and extensions to your existing range of products and services and also from innovations that cause a dramatic change in the course of the existing industry you operate within or from creating a new industry segment.

Vital to the growth of a business is knowledge and understanding of the needs and requirements of your customers, both in what they are looking for now and also in the future. As an organisation grows and more people are involved and more levels of structure are added, be it distinct departments within an organisation or different offices spread over a number of geographical locations, relaying information about new customer needs and new ideas created within the organisation, becomes increasingly difficult. Clear communication channels are required to disseminate and discuss ideas within and across the different departments and locations.

Ansoff matrix

One method by which to consider the possible ways in which you can seek to grow your business is to use the Ansoff matrix. The Ansoff matrix shows the four ways in which a business can grow and develop using the two dimensions: product/service development and extending the market or markets that a business sells its products and services into. The two dimensions produce the following four options:

➢ **Market penetration:** this option involves selling existing products to existing markets, such as selling more products to the same customers and by finding new customers in the existing markets in which you currently sell your products and services. Where the market is a mature or well developed one, with little year on year annual growth then finding new customers will usually involve winning customers away from competitors. As noted earlier, retaining existing customers can give growth options of selling more to them, such as by increasing the frequency that they purchase from you and increasing the quantity that they buy. A market penetration strategy is considered to be the least risky of the four options noted in the Ansoff matrix in terms of their being fewer unknowns as to, for example, customer knowledge about the value of your products and services and in the particular benefits which customers are looking for.

➢ **Market extension:** this option involves selling your existing product and service range into new markets or groups of customers. Market extension can include selling your products and services into new geographical locations, for example, extending your business from one with a local presence to perhaps one having a national or even global presence. Market extension can also mean finding new uses or applications for your products and/or services.

➢ **Product development:** this option involves developing or finding new products and services to sell to existing markets and customers. Product development could involve modifying existing products and services to improve those elements which are highly valued by customers.

➢ **Diversification:** this option involves developing new products for new markets or groups of customers. This option is the riskiest of the four options as you would be moving into uncharted territory, both in terms of the products you have to sell, your knowledge about potential customers and whether their initial interest would translate into actual sales.

```
                        Products/services

              Existing                    New

          ┌─────────────────┬─────────────────┐
          │                 │                 │
  Existing│     Market      │     Product     │
          │   Penetration   │   Development   │
          │                 │                 │
Markets   ├─────────────────┼─────────────────┤
          │                 │                 │
          │     Market      │ Diversification │
          │    Extension    │                 │
  New     │                 │                 │
          └─────────────────┴─────────────────┘

                       Ansoff matrix
```

Looking further at new markets and new customers

Further research into new customers and new markets can be found in the work of both J C Larreche and W C Kim and R Mauborgne, respectively. Their research and findings can help take your thoughts and ideas generation to a deeper level and can thus help you to find potential routes to radical growth opportunities for your business.

New customers

In The Momentum Effect, Larreche identifies four 'discovery paths', each of which can provide new and exciting "unlimited opportunities" for growth. Larreche provides the following summary of the four paths to identifying unsatisfied customer needs from which you may be able to identify, create and develop new products and services for your customers:

> ➤ **Knowing-doing discovery path**: contains unsatisfied customer needs that both the firm

and the customer are aware of. These unsatisfied needs are not exploited for two main reasons – unavailable technology and corporate apathy. One example of the success which can be achieved in the area of identifying and satisfying the unmet needs of customers is provided by Sir Richard Branson. He has created new businesses in a number of seemingly mature business sectors where growth opportunities, especially for a new business, would seem to be limited, such as airlines and financial products. In both of these businesses he has found ways to significantly improve on the quality of service that customers can expect and do consistently receive. In doing so he has created and developed both a happy and loyal customer base and also a number of highly successful and strong sustainable businesses.

- ➤ **Listening discovery path**: contains unsatisfied needs that some customers are aware of but the firm is not. Many entrepreneurs enter the world of business as frustrated customers with unsatisfied needs who develop solutions aimed at others like themselves. Most often, these needs are perceived and expressed by only a small number of leading customers. For example, many computer applications have been, and could be further, improved following users' feedback and suggestions that developers could not have imagined on their own.

- ➤ **Learning discovery path**: contains unsatisfied customer needs that the firm has unveiled of which the customer is unaware. Many new products fall into this category when they are first created – a firm knows that its customers have unsatisfied needs before they do. This was seen in past innovations, such as automobiles, computers and mobile phones. These growth opportunities lie in a firm's ability to educate and persuade customers about the value of a new offering. One example of a product in this category of unsatisfied customer needs was the Aeron chair when it was introduced in 1993. The chair is now regarded as a design classic but when it was first introduced into the market it looked too different from current office chairs on the market and sales were slow to take off. However, through educating prospective customers as to "the ergonomic brilliance behind its unusual looks" the chair went on to become a great success (Malcolm Gladwell, Blink and J C Larreche, The Momentum Effect).

- ➤ **White discovery path**: contains unsatisfied needs that no one has yet discovered but which may represent tremendous future business opportunities. This unexplored white space represents the ultimate frontier, and it includes nearly all the most powerful applications we take for granted today. At one point, neither their potential users nor their future creators imagined the enormous potential for spreadsheets, internet browsers or online telephony. This matrix is fluid – as new technologies progress and customer needs evolve, these hidden growth opportunities will be unveiled and move to one of the other 3 discovery paths.

Customers' Awareness of Their Unsatisfied Needs

	Known	Unknown
Known	Knowing-Doing Discovery Path	Learning Discovery Path
Unknown	Listening Discovery Path	White Discovery Path

The Firm's awareness of customers' Unsatisfied Needs

The insight discovery matrix (J C Larreche: The Momentum Effect)

Creating new markets

The models created in Blue Ocean Strategy by Kim and Mauborgne show you how you can seek to identify and to create your own new market sector for which there are no current existing competitors. In creating your own new market sector you are also creating your own rules. When you combine creating your own rules with also being able to create a product or service which has appeal to a mass market size customer base, then you can achieve a radically successful product or service and at the same time one that is exceptionally difficult for a competitor to enter your market space. For example, in 2003 Skype introduced the concept of high quality telephony over the internet free of charge to those customers who downloaded its free software. The combination of high quality and free Skype-to-Skype calls makes it incredibly difficult for a potential competitor to offer an improved product/service that would provide an effective competitor to Skype.

The starting point for identifying possible new markets is to alter your focus from looking purely at what currently exists, such as the products and services offered by you and your competitors and the existing customers of your industry, to a focus that looks at the opposite of what currently exists. That is, to focus on identifying the alternatives to using your product and service, for example, how else can customers get their problem solved or achieve the same outcome that they currently benefit from by using your product or service (or that of your competitors). In addition, also seek to identify who are the current non-customers of your industry and how might you be able to convert them into your customers.

One example cited by Kim and Mauborgne is Cirque du Soleil, who created a new market sector by combining the best elements, that is those valued highly by customers, from two 'industries': circuses and theatre. "Neither an ordinary circus nor a classic theatre production, Cirque du Soleil paid no heed to what the competition did. Instead of following the conventional logic of outpacing the competition by offering a better solution to the given problem of creating a circus with even greater fun and thrills – it sought to offer people the fun and thrill of the circus *and* the intellectual sophistication and artistic richness of the theatre at the same time; hence, it redefined the problem itself. By breaking the market boundaries of theatre and circus, Cirque du Soleil gained a new understanding not only of circus customers but also of circus non-customers: adult theatre customers. This led to a whole new circus concept". "In short, Cirque du Soleil offers the best of both circus and theatre and it has eliminated or reduced everything else. By offering unprecedented utility, Cirque du Soleil has created a blue ocean and has invented a new form of live entertainment, one that is markedly different from both traditional circus and theatre. At the same time, by eliminating many of the most costly elements of the circus, it has dramatically reduced its cost structure, achieving both differentiation and low cost. Le Cirque strategically priced its tickets against those of the theatre, lifting the price point of the circus industry by several multiples while still pricing its productions to capture the mass of adult customers, who were used to theatre prices."

The number of radical growth type products and services and markets are likely to increase going forwards, due to the increasingly globalised market place, where more people and businesses are connected with each other especially via the internet. The internet allows the rapid dissemination of ideas and for new products and services to reach a global market place in a very short space of time. The increasing speed with which ideas circulate also means that industries and business sectors will change more radically and rapidly than ever before. Rapidly changing and developing technology increasingly allows new entrepreneurs and entrepreneurs of small and medium sized businesses to compete effectively with larger and global corporate entities. The smaller sized business has many advantages including an entrepreneur who is closer to his/her customers and more able to understand their needs and who has the creativity and vision to come up with new ideas, products and services to bridge the gap where customers have unmet needs, together with an agile and nimble business structure which enables ideas to be converted into products and services on a much quicker time-scale than larger competitors.

System for collating information for research and development into growth opportunities

Vital to the growth of a business is knowledge and understanding of the needs and requirements of your customers and in being able to quickly identify, create and test new products and services which seek to satisfy the identified unmet needs of customers. Some of the aspects for creating a system for research and development into new products and services include:

➢ Having a system to collate information: information can include changes in the wider global environment, changes in technology, social and lifestyle changes, regulatory, political, environmental, economic changes; changes in your industry structure; on the activities and developments amongst your competitors; customer questionnaires and notes from your sales and marketing team giving information on insights derived from spending time with customers on how they use your products and services.

➢ Collating information is an ongoing activity and there should be a regular meeting system for discussing the ideas and information collated.

➢ Employing creative people, who are happy to work in an unstructured environment and who have a mindset of 'what is possible' and who seek to shape and identify possibilities rather than those who are happiest working in fixed and certain environments.

➢ Creative people can come from any part of your organisation. Ideas should be discussed by a group containing different departmental specialisms within your business.

- ➢ Giving space and time for creative thinkers to do their best work and to sift through information that has been collated from the variety of sources.

- ➢ Systematically recording new ideas and testing their viability for commercial success and recording why a new idea may work and not work.

- ➢ Having an efficient system that can move an idea quickly through the research, prototype testing and developmental stages.

Sources and further reading

Introduction–Chapter 4

Hamilton, R. (2006), Your Life Your Legacy – *An entrepreneurial guide to finding your flow*, Achievers International, SS Media Limited, Wallington, Surrey

Part 1

Bacharach, B. (2005), Values Based Financial Planning – The art of creating an inspiring financial strategy, Aim High Publishing, San Diego, CA

Canfield, J. and Switzer, J. (2005), The Success Principles – How to get from where you are to where you want to be, HarperElement, HarperCollins*Publishers* Ltd, London

De Martini, Dr J. F (2002), The Breakthrough Experience – A revolutionary new approach to personal transformation, Hay House UK Limited, London

Horovitz, J. and Ohlsson-Corboz, A-V. (2007), A Dream With A Deadline – Turning strategy into action, Prentice Hall Financial Times, Pearson Education Limited, Harlow

Kanter, R. M. (2004), Confidence – How winning streaks and losing streaks begin an d end, Random House, London

Maslow, A. H. (1999), Toward a Psychology of Being, 3rd edition, John Wiley & Sons Inc, New York, NY

Trump, D. J. and Zanker, B. (2007) – Think Big and Kick Ass In Business and Life, HarperCollins Publishers, New York, NY

Part 2

Branson, R. (2008), Business Stripped Bare – *Adventures of a global entrepreneur*, Virgin Books, London

Hatch, M.J and Schultz M (2008), Taking Brand Initiative - *How companies can align strategy, culture, and identity through corporate branding*, Jossey-Bass, San Francisco, CA

Johnson, G. and Scholes, K. (1999), Exploring Corporate Strategy,5th edition, Prentice Hall Europe, London

Olins, W (2008), The Brand Handbook, Thames & Hudson Limited, London

Sigurdsson, M. (2005), The Skype Brand – talk given at the Reboot Conference, Copenhagen, 16 June 2005.

Part 3

Churchill, N. C. and Lewis, V. L., (1983), The Five Stages of Small Business Growth, *Harvard Business Review.* May/June

Greiner, L. E. (1972), Evolution and revolution as organisations grow, Harvard Business Review, July/August

Kotter, J. P (1996), Leading Change, Harvard Business School Press, Boston, MA

Part 4

Ansoff, I. (1965), Corporate Strategy, McGraw-Hill, Maidenhead

Cram, T. (2006), Smarter Pricing – How to capture more value in your market, Prentice Hall Financial Times, Pearson Education Limited, Harlow

Gladwell, M. (2005), Blink – The power of thinking without thinking, Penguin Books Limited, London

Kim, W. C and Mauborgne, R (2005), Blue Ocean Strategy - *How to create uncontested market space and make the competition irrelevant*, Harvard Business School Press, Boston, MA

Larreche, J. C. (2008), The Momentum Effect - *How to ignite exceptional growth,* Wharton School Publishing, Pearson Education Limited, Harlow

Marn, M. and Rosiello, R. L (1992), Managing price, gaining profit, Harvard Business Review, September/October [1992 McKinsey survey]

Reichheld, F. and Sasser, W. Jr (1990) Zero defections: quality comes to services, Harvard Business Review (September/October) [Bain & Company]

www.ingramcontent.com/pod-product-compliance
Lightning Source LLC
Chambersburg PA
CBHW081139170526
45165CB00008B/2729